STUDY GUIDE

Amy L. Otto
Albion College

Pamela C. Regan
California State University, Los Angeles

ESSENTIALS
OF
PSYCHOLOGY

SAUL KASSIN

PEARSON
Prentice
Hall

Upper Saddle River, New Jersey 07458

© 2004 by PEARSON EDUCATION, INC.
Upper Saddle River, New Jersey 07458

ISBN 0-13-183639-0

Printed in the United States of America

TABLE OF CONTENTS

TO THE STUDENT

Welcome to psychology! This study guide was written to enhance your mastery of the material presented in the first edition of *Essentials of Psychology*, written by Dr. Saul Kassin. It will help you to identify important information, terms, and concepts; evaluate and test your own knowledge of the chapter material; and stimulate your thinking about various psychological phenomena. Please keep in mind that the study guide is not intended to serve as a substitute for the textbook. Rather, use the study guide to supplement and to measure what you've learned from the textbook and your lecture notes. Each study guide chapter corresponds to a chapter in your textbook and is divided into several different sections. Specifically:

Chapter Overview

This section briefly summarizes the material covered in the chapter and serves as a general introduction to the theory and research topics discussed by the author.

Chapter Outline

Human behavior and the human mind are remarkably diverse and complex. As a result, psychology – the discipline that seeks to understand human behavior and the human mind – is a big field with a constantly changing base of theoretical and empirical (research) knowledge. As you read through each chapter, you may find yourself thinking that it contains a lot of information; so much so that it's hard to grasp the major points or "big picture" without getting confused by all the details. The chapter outline consists of the major section headings and subheadings from the textbook and is designed to serve as an organizational plan that presents the larger structure of each chapter. You probably will find it useful to supplement this general outline with more detailed notes of your own, both from the textbook and from lecture.

Learning Objectives

Unlike the chapter outline, the learning objectives provide a *detailed* list of the concepts, ideas, and points that you can expect to learn from the textbook. To assist you in mastering the material, page references are placed beside each objective. Take the time to go over the objectives carefully before you read the chapter; this will prepare you for what to expect and also will serve to guide your note taking and reading. Then, make sure to return to the learning objectives after you have read the chapter; this will allow you to determine whether you indeed have mastered the essential concepts of the chapter. If there is an objective that still seems unclear, reread that particular section of text and/or ask your instructor.

Key Terms

This section lists and provides page references for all the key terms and concepts from each chapter. Unlike a traditional glossary, the key terms are presented in order of appearance in the chapter rather than alphabetically so that you can work your way through the text chapter from beginning to end instead of jumping from section to section and topic to topic. After reviewing, you should be able to define these terms in a few sentences (and provide examples, if appropriate).

Practice Multiple-Choice, True-False, and Key Concepts Matching Exercises

In addition to outlining the chapter and reviewing basic concepts, this study guide allows you to test your knowledge of each chapter in two different formats. The first consists of practice multiple-choice questions, true-false questions, and matching exercises drawn from the material presented in the text. These questions are designed to test your mastery of factual information, your conceptual understanding of particular ideas or theories, and your ability to apply what you have learned to novel situations not explicitly discussed in the textbook. The answers (and page references) to the practice questions are provided at the end of the study guide chapter.

Practice Essay Questions

Answering multiple-choice and true-false questions and matching key terms with their definitions are important ways through which you can test your knowledge of psychology. Writing about the concepts you have learned is another essential learning tool. This section of the study guide consists of practice essay questions that allow you to test your ability to describe, explain, and illustrate the ideas and points of each textbook chapter. Some basic guidelines are: (1) State your answers in a clear and concise manner; (2) avoid the use of colloquial or otherwise inappropriate language; (3) use examples when relevant; and (4) make an outline before you begin writing so that you know exactly what points you wish to make to your audience. A sample answer with page references has been provided for each practice essay question and placed at the end of the study guide chapter. Of course, because some of the questions ask you to supplement your definitions or descriptions of a particular concept or idea with examples drawn from personal experience, several different answers may be appropriate for any one question.

This study guide is intended to help you develop a knowledge base about psychology. If used in conjunction with a careful review of both the textbook and course lectures, it may enable you to increase your understanding of the material presented in each chapter. I hope that your text, course, and this study guide introduce you to the breadth and depth of the exciting, rapidly growing field of psychology, and I wish you much success with your studies.

CHAPTER 1

INTRODUCING PSYCHOLOGY AND ITS METHODS

CHAPTER OVERVIEW

The first part of this chapter introduces the field of psychology – its subject matter, its historical roots, and the individuals who established it as a legitimate arena of scientific inquiry. The major controversies that marked the beginnings of modern experimental psychology also are discussed, including the fundamental disagreement over what the "appropriate" goals, questions, and methods should be for this new science (e.g., subjective mental processes versus overt, observable behaviors). The text then explores some of the dramatic changes that have markedly altered the landscape of modern psychology, including the "cognitive revolution," the expansion of both basic and applied research areas, the issue of social responsibility, and increased diversity of members within the field. The second part of this chapter reviews the scientific methods used by psychologists in their quest to understand human behavior. Specifically, you will learn the differences among types of research settings (laboratory versus field), psychological measurements (self-reports, behavioral observations, and archival records), and research designs (descriptive, correlational, and experimental). This section concludes with a consideration of the ethical issues involved in using both humans and animals in psychological research. The remainder of the chapter focuses on the current state of the field of psychology, including a consideration of the two major perspectives that are used by contemporary psychologists to understand human behavior (biological and sociocultural perspectives).

CHAPTER OUTLINE

I. *What's Your Prediction* Thinking Like a Psychologist

II. What Is Psychology?

    A. Historical Roots
        1. Pioneers in the study of the mind
        2. The behaviorist alternative
        3. The "cognitive revolution"

    B. Expansion of Psychology's Horizons
        1. Psychology as a basic science
        2. Psychology as a responsive science
        3. Values, ethics, and social responsibility

    C. *Psychology and World Events* Psychological Consequences of Terrorism

D. *The Process of Discovery*   Gary L. Wells

E. A Diversity of Perspectives

III. Scientific Methods

A. The Research Process

B. Research Settings

C. Psychological Measurements
  1. Self-reports
  2. Behavioral observations
  3. Archival records

D. Research Designs
  1. Descriptive research
      a. Case studies
      b. Surveys
      c. Naturalistic observations
  2. Correlational studies
      a. Correlation and causation
  3. Experiments
      a. Control and comparison
      b. Random assignment
  4. Literature reviews

E. Ethical Considerations
  1. Ethics considerations in human research
  2. Ethics considerations in animal research

IV. Psychology Today

A. Biological Perspectives

B. Sociocultural Perspectives

V. Thinking Like a Psychologist About Psychology and Its Methods

LEARNING OBJECTIVES

By the time you have read and reviewed this chapter, you should be able to:

1. Define psychology and describe the three key elements in its definition (pp. 4-5).

2. Discuss the historical roots (in philosophy, physiology, and medicine) of modern-day psychology (p. 5).

3. Describe the contributions that Wilhelm Wundt and his students (Hall, Cattell, and Münsterberg) made to the field of psychology (p. 6). Compare the methods used by Wundt, James, and Freud to spark interest in psychology (pp. 6-7).

4. Describe the "behaviorist alternative" to the early focus on introspection and subjective experience (p. 8). Define behaviorism and compare this approach to the introspective approach favored by early psychologists (e.g., Wundt) (p. 8).

5. Define cognition and compare the behaviorist and cognitive approaches to understanding human behavior (p. 9). Describe three events or phenomena that incited the "cognitive revolution" (pp. 9-10).

6. Explain the difference between basic and applied research (pp. 10-11). Consider four ways in which psychology has developed since its original incarnation or conceptualization (pp. 10-11).

7. Describe the basic areas of specialization in psychology (i.e., biology, cognition/affect, human development, social psychology, and personality/clinical psychology) (pp. 11-12).

8. Consider how psychological theory and research can be used in the domains of health, education, business, law, the environment, and other applied areas (pp. 12-14).

9. Consider the ethical considerations faced by psychologists, including what degree of social responsibility researchers have when publishing controversial findings about human nature or behavior (pp. 13-15).

10. Discuss the ways in which the field of psychology has benefited from the growing diversity of its members (pp. 17-18).

11. Explain the concept of critical thinking and discuss the difference between a theory and a hypothesis (p. 19). Define the concept of operational definition and explain its role in hypothesis testing (pp. 20).

12. Distinguish between laboratory and field research settings (pp. 20-21).

13. Define and consider the advantages and disadvantages of each of the three types of psychological measurement (p. 21). Consider the difference between self-reports, behavioral observations, and archival records (pp. 21-23).

14. Describe the three types of research design: Descriptive studies, correlational studies, and experiments (pp. 23-29).

15. Explain the differences among case studies, surveys, and naturalistic observations (pp. 23-25).

16. Define the concept of correlation and explain the difference between a positive and a negative correlation (pp. 26-27). Explain the importance of the strength of a correlation coefficient (p. 26). Discuss the function of correlational studies and the types of conclusions that can be drawn from correlational evidence (p. 27).

17. Define the essential aspects of an experiment (pp. 27-29).

18. Describe a literature review (pp. 29-30). Consider the importance of replication and generalizability for any research finding (pp. 29-30).

19. Explain the three ethical concerns any researcher must address when conducting a study with human participants (p. 31). Consider the relations among deception, informed consent, and debriefing (pp. 31-32).

20. Consider reasons why psychologists must sometimes use animals in research (p. 32). Discuss the ethical obligation that researchers have when using animals (pp. 32-33).

21. Describe the influence of biological and sociocultural perspectives on modern psychology . (pp. 34-36).

KEY TERMS

The following key terms and concepts are featured in this chapter and are important for you to know. Write out definitions of each term and check your answers with the definitions in the text on the pages listed.

Psychology (p. 4)
Dualism (p. 5)
Introspection (p. 6)
Psychoanalysis (p. 7)
Behaviorism (p. 8)
Cognition (p. 9)
Basic research (p. 11)
Applied research (p. 11)

TEST QUESTIONS

Multiple-Choice Questions

Circle the correct choice for each question and compare your answers with those at the end of the Study Guide chapter.

1. According to your textbook, modern psychology is best understood as the scientific study of
    a. behavior and the mind.
    b. biological and sociocultural influences.
    c. conscious and unconscious mental states.
    d. mental disorders and psychoanalysis.

2. Which of the following examples are behaviors that psychologists might study?
    a. an eye blink
    b. smiling
    c. the decision to attend college
    d. All of the above

3. Which of the following disciplines influenced the development of modern psychology?
    a. philosophy
    b. physiology
    c. anthropology
    d. a and b

4. Wilhelm Wundt (1832-1920) used the method of _____ to study the human mind.
    a. hypnosis
    b. introspection
    c. psychoanalysis
    d. systems classification

5. Which early psychologist wrote the important textbook entitled *The Principles of Psychology?*
    a. James
    b. Freud
    c. Wundt
    d. Calkins

6. If the human mind is like an iceberg, then the very tip is the _____ part, and the huge area submerged under the water is the _____ part.
    a. penguin; whale
    b. unconscious; conscious
    c. conscious; unconscious
    d. surface; bottom

7. Dr. MustSee conducts his experiments by varying a stimulus in the environment and then observing a person's reaction. He thinks that motivations and feelings are interesting to talk about, but that such things cannot be studied scientifically and thus have no business in psychology. Dr. MustSee probably is best described as a
   a. behaviorist.
   b. philosopher.
   c. cognitive psychologist.
   d. psychoanalyst.

8. Which of the following developments contributed to the "cognitive revolution"?
   a. the invention of the computer
   b. Piaget's studies on the development of thinking in children
   c. developments in the study of language
   d. All of the above

9. The goal of basic research is to
   a. discover general principles of human behavior.
   b. solve practical problems.
   c. examine human behavior in real-world settings.
   d. All of the above

10. Which of the following topics would be of interest to a biological psychologist?
   a. the situations that influence the expression of aggression
   b. the evolutionary origins of aggression
   c. the cross-cultural experience and expression of anger
   d. treatment programs for violent offenders

11. Psychologists develop theories from which of the following sources?
   a. research findings
   b. personal experience or observation
   c. other theories
   d. All of the above

12. If you were interested in studying the development of dominance hierarchies in wolf packs, the best type of measurement to use would be
   a. behavioral observation.
   b. self-reports.
   c. archival records.
   d. meta-analysis.

13. A psychologist is interested in studying beliefs about the elderly. To examine trends in stereotypes of the aged, she collects and examines portraits and drawings of elderly men and women engaged in a variety of activities across several historical eras. This psychologist is relying upon _____ for her study.
   a. self-report
   b. historical trend analysis
   c. archival records
   d. behavioral observation

14. In seeking to understand the factors that contribute to divorce, a researcher interviews a divorced couple at great length. Each member of the couple is asked to provide a detailed description of the reasons the marriage failed. This example describes a(n)
   a. meta-analysis.
   b. correlational study.
   c. experiment.
   d. case study.

15. Which of the following are examples of descriptive research designs?
   a. case study
   b. naturalistic observation
   c. survey
   d. All of the above

16. Wendy notices that the more time she spends reviewing her psychology text and lecture notes, the higher her quiz scores tend to be. Her review time and her quiz scores are
   a. randomly related.
   b. positively correlated.
   c. negatively correlated.
   d. causally connected.

17. One of the most significant disadvantages of a correlational study is that it
   a. is unable to examine the relationship between behaviors.
   b. has limited generalizability.
   c. cannot be used to explain the causes of behaviors.
   d. cannot be used to predict behavior.

18. Mark is interested in examining the relation between shyness and dating experience. He believes that shy people will have less dating experience than non-shy people. To test his hypothesis, Mark administers the "Adult Shyness Scale" to a sample of college students, and then asks them to report on the number of first dates they have had in the last year. He finds a negative relationship between shyness level and number of first dates. What can Mark conclude?
   a. Shyness causes dating anxiety.
   b. Dating experience is a function of shyness.
   c. People who date a lot become less shy.
   d. None of the above

Questions 19-21 refer to the following scenario. Read it carefully!

Emma is working on her senior thesis. She thinks that couples experience less physiological arousal when they are having a "positive" discussion than when they are having a "negative" discussion (in other words, type of discussion affects physiological arousal). To test her hypothesis, she asks 20 married couples to come into the laboratory. Upon their arrival, the couples complete a "relationship satisfaction survey." Then, the couples are hooked up to machines that record their physiological arousal. Emma randomly assigns 10 of the couples to discuss an area of conflict in their relationships while the machines measure their heart rate and blood pressure. The other 10 couples are randomly assigned to discuss an area of pleasure in their relationship and their heart rate and blood pressure are assessed. Emma finds that the first group (conflict discussion) becomes more physiologically aroused during their discussions than the second group (pleasure discussion).

19. Describe Emma's study. What kind of research design, psychological measurement, and research setting has she used?
   a. descriptive; self-report; field
   b. experimental; self-report; field
   c. correlational; behavioral observation; laboratory
   d. experimental; behavioral observation; laboratory

20. What is the independent variable in this study?
   a. the type of relationship the couples have
   b. the couple's satisfaction level
   c. the physiological arousal experienced by the couples
   d. the type of discussion in which the couples engage

21. What is the dependent variable in this study?
   a. the type of relationship the couples have
   b. the couple's satisfaction level
   c. the physiological arousal experienced by the couples
   d. the type of discussion in which the couples engage

9

22. When all the participants have an equal probability of being placed in either the experimental or control group, the procedure is called
    a. random sampling.
    b. random assignment.
    c. representative sampling.
    d. manipulation.

23. Matt has read Emma's published study. For his thesis, he decides to conduct a nearly identical study to see if the initial findings can be repeated. Matt is testing the _____ of Emma's study.
    a. replicability
    b. manipulability
    c. generalizability
    d. proof

24. Matt then decides to conduct the same study again, but this time using much older couples and a different measure of arousal. Matt is now testing the _____ of Emma's study.
    a. replicability
    b. manipulability
    c. generalizability
    d. proof

25. The set of procedures used to examine a research question by combining the results from multiple studies is called
    a. statistics.
    b. meta-analysis.
    c. literature review.
    d. correlation.

26. Ethical concerns raised by research involving the use of human participants include which of the following?
    a. the participant's right to privacy.
    b. possible harm caused by experimental procedures.
    c. the use of deception.
    d. All of the above

27. Informed consent refers to
    a. revealing in advance that an experiment will involve deception.
    b. informing participants that they are required to complete an experiment once it begins.
    c. fully explaining the experimental manipulation prior to participation.
    d. None of the above

28. Your textbook author describes an example from his own experience as a research participant in which he agreed to be in an IQ study. He took a test and was told that his score was quite low, in the 25th percentile. On his way out, feeling bad about his low IQ, he was approached by a student who asked him to help out by completing a survey. The experimenter then appeared and revealed that there was no survey and the IQ feedback had been false. The study actually was designed to examine whether positive or negative experiences could influence helping behavior. This example demonstrates
    a. random assignment and debriefing.
    b. informed consent and the right to privacy.
    c. deception and debriefing.
    d. deception and the right to withdraw.

29. Animal researchers have a moral obligation to do which of the following?
    a. minimize pain and suffering
    b. ensure that animals receive adequate food and water
    c. ensure that animals receive adequate shelter and medical treatment
    d. All of the above

30. Psychologists who evaluate the generality of theories of human behavior by comparing people from different world regions are conducting _____ research.
    a. evolutionary
    b. cross-cultural
    c. multicultural
    d. behavioral neuroscience

True-False Questions

Indicate which of the following statements are true or false, and compare your answers with those at the end of the chapter.

T F   1. The term "mind" in modern-day psychology refers only to conscious mental states.

T F   2. Behaviorism is concerned with mental processes that connect a stimulus with a response.

T F   3. Basic research is used to test theories and discover general laws of human behavior.

T F   4. Some psychologists develop their theories of human behavior by examining existing theories and research.

T F   5. A major disadvantage of self-report measurements is that people may distort their responses.

T F 6. Behavioral observation can never be used to study subjective experiences like curiosity.

T F 7. Case studies have played an influential role in the history of psychology.

T F 8. Correlational studies provide an effective means of examining the causal relationship between two variables.

T F 9. It is possible to manipulate more than one independent variable in an experiment.

T F 10. One well-designed study can prove a hypothesis.

Key Concepts Matching Exercises

Exercise #1: Historical Foundations

Match the key people on the left with their contributions to psychology.

_____ 1. Descartes

_____ 2. Piaget

_____ 3. Freud

_____ 4. Calkins

_____ 5. Hippocrates

_____ 6. Kraepelin

_____ 7. Watson

_____ 8. Wundt

_____ 9. Hall

_____ 10. James

a. founder of modern medicine

b. founded the APA

c. followed the philosophical position known as dualism

d. wrote the two-volume *Principles of Psychology*

e. established the field of psychoanalysis

f. viewed psychology as the study of observable behavior

g. created the first psychology laboratory

h. first woman president of the APA

i. developed the first system for classifying mental disorders

j. developed an influential theory of cognitive development

#2: Scientific Methods

Match the key concepts on the left with the definitions on the right.

_____ 1. Archival measures

_____ 2. Case study

_____ 3. Correlation

_____ 4. Dependent variable

_____ 5. Replication

_____ 6. Experiment

_____ 7. Hypothesis

_____ 8. Field research

_____ 9. Survey

_____ 10. Independent variable

_____ 11. Theory

_____ 12. Random assignment

a. statistical measure of the relation between two variables

b. used to describe the behavior of populations

c. examines cause-and-effect relations

d. process of repeating a study

e. testable prediction about the relationship between two or more variables

f. what is manipulated by the researcher

g. in-depth examination of one individual

h. what is measured by the researcher

i. research conducted in "real world" settings

j. set of principles that describes, explains, and predicts a phenomenon

k. process of arbitrarily putting participants into the experimental or control groups

l. used to examine historical trends in human behavior

Essay Questions

Write out answers to the following brief essay questions. Compare your responses with the sample answers at the end of the Study Guide chapter.

1. Your textbook author argues that psychology has "a long past but a short history." Explain what this statement means, using your knowledge of the historical foundations of modern psychology.

2. One of the most important events that shaped (and still is shaping) the face of modern psychology is the "cognitive revolution." What is cognition, and what is meant by the term "cognitive revolution"? What major events contributed to the cognitive revolution?

3. Upon receiving your Ph.D. in Psychology, you are hired by the owners of a large retail toy company to assist in the development of a new set of playground equipment that will be used in parks throughout the area. As a first step, you decide to explore the kinds of activities children actually engage in while playing with each other in park-like settings. Explain the difference between laboratory research and field research and provide an example of how you would use each setting to examine your research question. What are the advantages and disadvantages of each research setting? Is one research setting "better" than the other?

4. Many psychologists collect behavioral data from the participants in their studies. What is "behavioral observation?" What are some advantages and disadvantages of using this type of measurement?

5. What is a survey? Define this concept and give an example of a survey study or question that might be answered by a survey. What factors are particularly important for psychologists who use surveys to consider? Use relevant examples when necessary.

TEST SOLUTIONS

Multiple-Choice Solutions

1. a (pp. 4-5)
2. d (pp. 4-5)
3. d (p. 5)
4. b (p. 6)
5. a (p. 6)
6. c (p. 7)
7. a (p. 8)
8. d (pp. 9-10)
9. a (p. 11)
10. b (p. 12)

11. d (p. 19)
12. a (p. 22)
13. c (pp. 22-23)
14. d (p. 23)
15. d (p. 23)
16. b (p. 26)
17. c (p. 27)
18. d (pp. 26-27)
19. d (pp. 20-27)
20. d (p. 27)

21. c (p. 27)
22. b (pp. 28-29)
23. a (p. 29)
24. c (p. 29)
25. b (pp. 29-30)
26. d (p. 31)
27. d (p. 31)
28. c (p. 31)
29. d (pp. 32-33)
30. b (p. 35)

True-False Solutions

1. F (p. 5)
2. F (p. 8)
3. T (p. 11)
4. T (p. 19)
5. T (p. 21)

6. F (p. 22)
7. T (p. 23)
8. F (p. 27)
9. T (p. 28)
10. F (p. 29)

Key Concepts Matching Solutions

Exercise #1

1. c
2. j
3. e
4. h
5. a
6. i
7. f
8. g
9. b
10. d

Exercise #2

1. l
2. g
3. a
4. h
5. d
6. c
7. e
8. i
9. b
10. f
11. j
12. k

Essay Solutions

1. As a discipline, psychology has its roots in much older disciplines (in other words, psychology has a long past). For example, the ancient Greek philosophers Socrates, Plato, and Aristotle wrote a number of treatises about aspects of human behavior and the mind, including pleasure and pain, the five sensory systems, imagination, and motivation. Similarly, Hippocrates and Galen (early physicians) formed theories about human behavior, consciousness, and personality. More recently (but still prior to psychology's actual "founding"), physiologists like Helmholtz and Fechner began to study the brain and the processes of sensation and perception and medical professionals like Kraepelin and Charcot began to classify and treat mental disorders. However, it was only in the late 1800s that modern experimental psychology was born when Wilhelm Wundt established the first laboratory specifically dedicated to the study of the human mind. Thus, psychology has a long past but a short history. (pp. 5-7)

2. Cognition refers to the mental processes that occur or intervene between a stimulus and a response (in other words, subjective phenomena like expectations, feelings, and images that lie between an environmental stimulus and our response to that stimulus). The term "cognitive revolution" refers to the reemergence of subjective, nonobservable phenomena (like expectations and affect) as suitable topics for scientific inquiry (remember that behaviorism and its emphasis on observable, overt behavior and stimulus-response patterns was the dominant perspective at the time; the cognitive revolution reinstated the primacy of the organism and the mind that lie between stimulus and response). (p. 10)

Three events contributed to the cognitive revolution. The first was the invention of the computer; computers provided a new model for the human mind (an information-processing model). A second factor that contributed to the cognitive revolution was the cognitive theory of Piaget, who studied the development of thinking and reasoning in children. Piaget's writings were translated into English in the 1950s and 1960s, and they provided another source of inspiration for researchers interested in cognition. Finally, new research on language development demonstrated that language acquisition is not controlled by laws of learning (the behaviorist perspective) but rather is a function of specialized cognitive structures that are "hard-wired" into the human brain. (p. 10)

3. Laboratory research involves collecting data from participants in a controlled environment in which they can be carefully observed. In this situation, you might recreate a park-like setting in the lab, bring children into this setting, videotape their interactions with each other, and then analyze their behavior (e.g., count the number of times children enter into solo vs. group activity). The advantage of this type of research is that it offers a lot of environmental control (you can monitor all aspects of the children's behavior). The disadvantage is that a laboratory setting is artificial and may actually cause participants to engage in unusual behavior. If the room in which children are playing is not like an actual playground, how do we know if we are really measuring "playground behavior?" (p. 20)

The alternative to laboratory research is field research – this is research conducted in actual, real-world locations. In this situation, you could go to a playground that contains a mix of toys and children, observe several of these children over a specified period of time, and record various activities in which they engage. The advantage is that you would gain insight into what actually occurs in a park-like setting; the disadvantage is that you lose control over the situation and cannot precisely analyze every single aspect of the children's behavior. (pp. 20-21)

One setting is not necessarily better than the other. Both have advantages and disadvantages. Consequently, the best approach for answering any research question is to use both laboratory and field settings.

4. Behavioral observations involve observing a participant's behavior firsthand, either openly or covertly. This type of measurement is the major alternative to self-report. An advantage of behavioral observation is that it allows psychologists to measure behavior objectively without relying on self-report data that may be distorted or inaccurate. For example, people may be unwilling to provide a truthful description of their drinking behavior; thus, a researcher who observes people in a bar may obtain a much more accurate assessment of drinking behavior than one who relies upon people's self-reports. The problem with using behavioral observation is that inner states (like feelings of anger or love) cannot be directly observed from behavior. Also, people may behave differently if they realize that they are being measured (for example, bar patrons might alter their drinking behavior if they become aware that a researcher is observing them). (p. 22)

5. Surveys are considered one type of descriptive research design. Their purpose is to describe an entire population by looking at many cases (p. 24). For example, a psychologist might investigate the percentage of husbands and wives who have an affair by calling 10,000 individuals and asking those who are married to provide an answer to this question.

There are two main factors that should be of concern to psychologists who use this research design. The first involves sampling issues (i.e., who the respondents are). To describe any group (like the population of married people), the researcher selects a subset of that group (the sample, or 10,000 married people). For a survey to be accurate, the sample has to be as representative of the larger population as possible. In this case, it is important that the 10,000 married people surveyed by the researcher be randomly selected from the larger population so that they resemble that population in terms of age, race/ethnicity, income, and so on. If the researcher has only surveyed upper-income, middle-aged individuals, the results may not tell us much about the faithfulness of married people in general. Second, the researcher must consider how he or she words or frames the research questions. For example, respondents might provide quite different answers to the question, "Have you ever had an extramarital relationship?" than they would to the question, "Have you ever deliberately violated your sacred marriage vows by cheating on your beloved spouse?" (p. 24).

17

CHAPTER 2

BEHAVIORAL NEUROSCIENCE

CHAPTER OVERVIEW

This chapter focuses upon behavioral neuroscience, an area of psychology concerned with exploring the biological roots of human experience. Specifically, your text begins with an overview of the body's communication systems – the nervous system and the endocrine system – and the behaviors affected by different parts of those interconnected systems. The chapter then examines the structure and function of neurons (basic building blocks of the nervous system) and how neural communication influences our behavior through the release of neurotransmitters. The brain is the next topic of discussion. Your textbook author presents research methods available for studying brain activity and function (i.e., case study, experimental interventions, electrical recordings, imaging), discusses the various regions of the brain and the behaviors and events that each regulates, and explores the "split-brain" phenomenon and the notion of cerebral lateralization (brain function asymmetry). The chapter ends with an exploration of several topics that lie in the intersection between basic behavioral neuroscience and applied areas of psychology – plasticity, neurogenesis, neural transplantation, and head injury.

CHAPTER OUTLINE

I. *What's Your Prediction* One Brain or Two?

II. The Body's Communication Networks

    A. The Nervous System

    B. The Endocrine System

III. The Neuron

    A. Structure of the Neuron

    B. The Neuron in Action

    C. How Neurons Communicate

    D. Neurotransmitters

IV. The Brain

    A. Tools of Behavioral Neuroscience
        1. Clinical case studies
        2. Experimental interventions
        3. Electrical recordings
        4. Brain-imaging techniques

    B. Regions of the Brain
        1. The brainstem
        2. The limbic system
            a. The thalamus
            b. The amygdala
            c. The hippocampus
            d. The hypothalamus
        3. The cerebral cortex
            a. Sensory and motor areas
            b. Association areas
            c. Language areas
            d. The integrated brain

    C. The Split Brain
        1. Split-brain studies
        2. How split-brain patients adapt
        3. Cerebral lateralization

    D. *Psychology and Health* Being Left-Handed in a Right-Handed World

    E. *The Process of Discovery* Michael S. Gazzaniga

V. Prospects for the Future

    A. The Brain's Capacity for Growth and Reorganization
        1. The benefit of plasticity: Growth through experience
        2. The cost of plasticity: The case of the phantom limb

    B. Repairing the Damaged Brain: New Frontiers
        1. Neurogenesis
        2. Neural transplantation

    C. *Psychology and Sports* Head Injury in Contact Sports

VI. Thinking Like a Psychologist About Behavioral Neuroscience

LEARNING OBJECTIVES

By the time you have read and reviewed this chapter, you should be able to:

1. Discuss the story of Phineas Gage and what his case revealed about the human brain and nervous system (pp. 42-43).

2. Distinguish among the various parts of the nervous system (pp. 44-45). Define the functions controlled by the central and peripheral nervous systems and list the different parts of these systems (pp. 44-45).

3. Define the elements and functions of the endocrine system (pp. 45-46). Discuss how the nervous and endocrine systems communicate (pp. 45-46).

4. Explain what a neuron is and list and define the different types of neurons (p. 46). Explain the function and the structures of a neuron (p. 48).

5. Explain how neurons communicate (pp. 49-50). Discuss the relationship between neurotransmitters and behavior (pp. 50-52).

6. Consider the various "tools" that psychologists have at their disposal for studying brain activity and function (pp. 52-56).

7. Explain the difference between case studies, experimental interventions, electrical recordings, and brain-imaging techniques (pp. 53-56). State the advantages and disadvantages of each method and what each reveals about the human brain.

8. Describe the regions of the human brain (pp. 56-63).

9. List the structures that comprise the brainstem and the function of each one (pp. 56-58).

10. List the structures of the limbic system and the function of each one (pp. 58-59).

11. Explain the differences in the cerebral cortex found in more complex compared to less complex species (pp. 59-60). List and describe the functional regions of the cortex (pp. 60-63).

12. Distinguish between the somatosensory and the motor cortex, and explain the functions controlled by each (pp. 61-62).

13. Describe the association cortex (p. 62).

14. Explain the difference between the two language areas of the cortex (Broca's area and Wernicke's area) (p. 62).

15. Discuss whether the functions of the human brain are localized or whether the brain operates as an integrated system (p. 63).

16. Discuss the relation between handedness and health. Compare and contrast the longevity hypothesis and the modification hypothesis (pp. 64-65).

17. Explain why split-brain surgery has sometimes been done (p. 66). Discuss the "division of labor" in the brain and how this affects split-brain patients (pp. 66-67, 69).

18. Consider the case for cerebral lateralization (pp. 69-70).

19. Define the concept of plasticity (p. 71) and discuss whether the adult human brain can be changed through enrichment experiences (pp. 71-72). Consider the ways in which plasticity may produce harmful outcomes (p. 73).

20. Define the concept of neurogenesis and discuss whether this process occurs in the brains of adult humans (pp. 73-74).

21. Discuss the signs of a concussion and the ways in which head trauma to athletes can be minimized (pp. 74-75).

22. Consider developments in our ability to repair brain damage (e.g., neural grafts) (pp. 75-76). Discuss the ethical dilemmas raised by those developments (p. 76).

KEY TERMS

The following key terms and concepts are featured in this chapter and are important for you to know. Write out definitions of each term and check your answers with the definitions in the text on the pages listed.

Central nervous system (CNS) (p. 44)
Peripheral nervous system (PNS) (p. 44)
Somatic nervous system (p. 44)
Autonomic nervous system (p. 44)
Sympathetic nervous system (p. 45)
Parasympathetic nervous system (p. 45)
Endocrine system (p. 45)
Hormones (p. 45)
Pituitary gland (p. 45)
Neurons (p. 46)
Sensory neurons (p. 46)
Motor neurons (p. 46)
Interneurons (p. 46)
Neural networks (p. 47)

TEST QUESTIONS

Multiple-Choice Questions

Circle the correct choice for each question and compare your answers with those at the end of the Study Guide chapter.

1. Which of the following items does not belong with the rest?
   a. central nervous system
   b. peripheral nervous system
   c. somatic nervous system
   d. autonomic nervous system

2. Which of the following items is out of place?
   a. parasympathetic system
   b. autonomic nervous system
   c. somatic nervous system
   d. sympathetic system

3. Which one of the following experiences is regulated or controlled by the autonomic nervous system?
   a. the taste of a lemon
   b. the sound of a bird singing
   c. the beating of a heart
   d. the movement of a runner's legs

4. The endocrine system is involved in the regulation of human
   a. growth.
   b. sexual development.
   c. metabolism.
   d. All of the above

5. Joanne is getting ready for her morning run. While she is sitting on her porch tying her shoes, her neighbor calls out a greeting. Joanne raises her head and replies, "Good morning!" The type of neuron that enables Joanne to tie her shoes is _____; the type of neuron that enables her to hear her neighbor's greeting is _____.
   a. sensory; motor
   b. motor; sensory
   c. sensory; interneuron
   d. motor; motor

6. The part of a neuron that receives impulses from organs or other neurons is called
    a. the dendrite.
    b. the axon.
    c. the soma.
    d. the nucleus.

7. The purpose of the myelin sheath surrounding a neuron's axon is
    a. to insulate the axon.
    b. to speed up the movement of electrical impulses.
    c. to prevent leakage of electrical impulses.
    d. All of the above

8. Action potentials have which of the following characteristics?
    a. they are triggered any time a neuron is stimulated
    b. they are an all-or-none response
    c. they are reversible
    d. All of the above

9. Neurotransmitters have been implicated in a number of human experiences, including
    a. depression.
    b. intelligence.
    c. growth.
    d. socioeconomic status.

10. Suppose that you are a researcher at a toxicology lab. One day, you accidentally inject yourself with curare, a poison that blocks the release of acetylcholine in the nervous system. What will you experience?
    a. violent muscle contractions
    b. hand tremors
    c. paralysis
    d. sleeplessness

11. Suppose that you receive immediate treatment for your curare poisoning, but the very next day you accidentally inject yourself with a solution that causes the release of serotonin. What will you feel now?
    a. depressed
    b. sleepy
    c. schizophrenic
    d. anxious

12. A teacher takes his class on a field trip to see the famous "Dr. Fantastik." For a small fee, Dr. Fantastik carefully examines the skull of each child and then makes a pronouncement about the characteristics that child possesses. The notion that physical features of the skull correspond to psychological characteristics is known as
    a. pseudoscience.
    b. phrenology.
    c. phenomenology.
    d. scientology.

13. Behavioral neuroscientists utilize a variety of research methods in their attempts to understand the human brain. Examples of experimental interventions include
    a. the creation of brain lesions.
    b. the administration of drugs.
    c. electrical brain stimulation.
    d. All of the above

14. Some brain-imaging techniques can be used to map brain activity as it actually occurs over time. These techniques include
    a. CT scan.
    b. PET scan.
    c. functional MRI.
    d. b and c

15. The _____ helps regulate "primitive" life-support functions like breathing, whereas the _____ controls "higher" mental processes like complex learning.
    a. brainstem; cortex
    b. limbic system; cortex
    c. brainstem; limbic system
    d. cortex; limbic system

16. A person who has difficulty focusing his or her attention and who is experiencing sleep disruptions may have sustained damage to the _____.
    a. medulla
    b. reticular formation
    c. cerebellum
    d. pons

17. Bart was in an accident that caused him to sustain some minor damage to his limbic system. The accident seems to have affected his ability to form new memories. What part of the limbic system is likely to have been involved?
    a. the amygdala
    b. the hypothalamus
    c. the hippocampus
    d. the thalamus

18. The limbic system plays an important role in regulating
    a. motivation.
    b. memory.
    c. emotion.
    d. All of the above

19. Your textbook author believes that "if you had to sacrifice an ounce of brain tissue, you wouldn't want to take it from the hypothalamus." Why does he make this statement?
    a. The hypothalamus regulates higher thought processes.
    b. Stimulation of the hypothalamus causes pleasure.
    c. The hypothalamus helps us to retrieve important personal memories.
    d. Stimulation of the hypothalamus releases acetylcholine.

20. Which of the following statements about the cerebral cortex is accurate?
    a. The cerebral cortex is the innermost covering of the brain.
    b. The cerebral cortex is present in all mammals except dolphins and whales.
    c. The cerebral cortex constitutes about 10 percent of the human brain.
    d. None of the above

21. The _____ lobe in the back of the brain is the primary visual cortex.
    a. temporal
    b. occipital
    c. frontal
    d. parietal

22. The _____ the need for precise control over a body part, the _____ is its area in the motor cortex.
    a. greater; smaller
    b. smaller; larger
    c. greater; larger
    d. There is no relation between need for control over a body part and size of its motor cortex area.

23. The _____ cortex communicates with the sensory cortex and the motor cortex and houses the brain's higher mental processes.
    a. somatosensory
    b. association
    c. broca
    d. motor

24. Both Laurie and Gene have experienced brain damage. Laurie does not understand what people are saying to her, but she speaks in complete sentences and produces fluent, grammatical speech. Gene, on the other hand, understands what other people are saying to him, but he is unable to produce complete, grammatical sentences. Ann most likely has sustained damage to _____; Gene most likely has sustained damage to

    _____.
    a. Broca's area; Wernicke's area
    b. Wernicke's area; Broca's area
    c. the left hemisphere; the right hemisphere
    d. the temporal lobe; the frontal lobe

25. The key language centers in the brain are located in the _____.
    a. corpus callosum
    b. occipital lobe
    c. right hemisphere
    d. left hemisphere

26. George has severe epilepsy. One possible way of reducing the severity of his seizures is to sever the _____.
    a. limbic system
    b. frontal lobe
    c. corpus callosum
    d. Wernicke area

27. The primary function of the corpus callosum is to
    a. allow the two cerebral hemispheres to communicate.
    b. control the comprehension and production of language.
    c. produce emotional responses.
    d. regulate the body's hormone levels.

28. A split-brain patient is shown a slide of the words <u>puppy</u> <u>dog</u> in such a way that her right visual field (the left hemisphere of the brain) sees only the word <u>dog</u> and her left visual field (the right hemisphere of the brain) sees only the word <u>puppy</u>. When asked to tell what she sees, what will she say?
    a. puppy
    b. dog
    c. puppy dog
    d. dog puppy

29. Research on cerebral lateralization suggests that the right hemisphere plays a vital role in
    a. visual-spatial tasks.
    b. music.
    c. face recognition.
    d. All of the above

30. Living in an "enriched" environment may produce
   a. dendritic growth.
   b. hemispheric specialization.
   c. neural grafts.
   d. split-brain syndrome.

True-False Questions

Indicate which of the following statements are true or false, and compare your answers with those at the end of the chapter.

T F   1. Neural impulses are generally more rapid than hormonal messages.

T F   2. The nervous system and endocrine system are in constant communication.

T F   3. Each neuron is linked with no more than five other neurons.

T F   4. Neural communication involves both chemical and electrical processes.

T F   5. Each neurotransmitter is capable of binding only to certain receptors.

T F   6. Phrenology is one of the primary methods utilized by modern neuroscientists.

T F   7. In general, the more complex the species, the more convoluted the cortex.

T F   8. Most psychologists prefer to divide the areas of the brain according to function rather than to actual physical region.

T F ·9. Research on language disorders suggests that there is only one distinct cortical center for language.

T F 10. Current evidence on cerebral lateralization indicates that the left and right hemispheres of the brain are specialized to process different information.

Key Concepts Matching Exercises

Exercise #1: The Nervous System

Match the key concepts on the left with the definitions on the right.

_____ 1. Central nervous system   a. connects sensory organs and skin to the CNS

_____ 2. Somatic nervous system   b. connects the CNS to involuntary muscles and organs

_____ 3. Endocrine system   c. the body's "Department of Peace"

_____ 4. Parasympathetic division   d. consists of the brain and spinal cord

_____ 5. Autonomic nervous system   e. collection of ductless glands that secrete hormones

_____ 6. Sympathetic division   f. the body's "Department of War"

Exercise #2: The Neuron

Match the key concepts on the left with the definitions on the right.

_____ 1. Soma   a. the "glue" that provides neurons with structural support, nutrients, and insulation

_____ 2. Axon   b. functions as the neuron's "antennae"

_____ 3. Glial cell   c. fatty substance that insulates the axon and speeds neural communication

_____ 4. Synapse   d. all-or-nothing burst of information that travels in the form of electrical energy

_____ 5. Interneuron   e. knoblike "tips" that contain neurotransmitters

_____ 6. Dendrite   f. fiber that sends information through one neuron to another

_____ 7. Axon terminal   g. the cell body of a neuron

_____ 8. Myelin sheath   h. narrow gap between neighboring neurons

_____ 9. Neurotransmitter   i. links sensory and motor neurons

_____ 10. Action potential   j. chemical substance that transmits information from one neuron to another

Exercise #3: The Brain

Match the key concepts on the left with the definitions on the right.

_____ 1. Brainstem   a. plays a key role in speech production

_____ 2. Reticular formation   b. damage to this structure impairs coordination
                                     and balance

_____ 3. Cerebellum   c. is involved in the formation of new memories

_____ 4. Limbic system   d. portion of the brain that represents all 600
                                     muscles in the human body

_____ 5. Hippocampus   e. plays a key role in speech comprehension

_____ 6. Cerebral cortex   f. netlike group of neurons that control sleep,
                                     arousal, and attention

_____ 7. Motor cortex   g. "bridge" that connects the two hemispheres

_____ 8. Broca's area   h. regulates emotion, motivation, and memory

_____ 9. Wernicke's area   i. outermost covering of the brain

_____ 10. Corpus callosum   j. regulates primitive behaviors like breathing

Essay Questions

Write out answers to the following brief essay questions. Compare your responses with the sample answers at the end of the Study Guide chapter.

1. The pituitary gland has been called the "master gland" of the endocrine system. Why?

2. Discuss three types of experimental intervention that are commonly used by behavioral neuroscientists to explore the functions of the brain.

3. Is there a link between the amygdala and aggression? Explain why this part of the limbic system has been called an "aggression center."

4. Discuss the research on the split-brain phenomenon and cerebral lateralization to support the statement, "Each side of the brain is its own mind."

5. What is plasticity? Define this concept and discuss whether the adult brain can be altered by environmental stimulation.

TEST SOLUTIONS

Multiple-Choice Solutions

1. a (p. 44)
2. c (p. 45)
3. c (p. 45)
4. d (p. 45)
5. b (p. 46)
6. a (p. 48)
7. d (p. 48)
8. b (p. 49)
9. a (p. 50)
10. c (p. 51)

11. b (p. 50)
12. b (p. 52)
13. d (p. 53)
14. d (pp. 54-55)
15. a (p. 56)
16. b (p. 56)
17. c (p. 58)
18. d (p. 58)
19. b (p. 59)
20. d (pp. 59-60)

21. b (p. 60)
22. c (p. 61)
23. b (p. 62)
24. b (p. 62)
25. d (p. 63)
26. c (p. 66)
27. a (p. 66)
28. b (p. 67)
29. d (p. 69)
30. a (pp. 71-72)

True-False Solutions

1. T (p. 45)
2. T (p. 46)
3. F (p. 46)
4. T (pp. 49-50)
5. T (p. 50)

6. F (pp. 52-53)
7. T (p. 59)
8. T (p. 60)
9. F (p. 62)
10. T (pp. 69-70)

Key Concepts Matching Solutions

Exercise #1

1. d
2. a
3. e
4. c
5. b
6. f

Exercise #2

1. g
2. f
3. a
4. h
5. i
6. b
7. e
8. c
9. j
10. d

Exercise #3

1. j
2. f
3. b
4. h
5. c
6. i
7. d
8. a
9. e
10. g

Essay Solutions

1. The pituitary gland is a small but powerful structure that sits at the base of the brain. When it receives the "go ahead," this gland releases a hormone that in turn stimulates the production and release of hormones in other endocrine glands. These hormones flow back to the brain, which then informs the hypothalamus to ask the pituitary for more or less hormone production. Thus, the pituitary gland is the master gland! (pp. 45-46)

2. One experimental intervention involves purposefully disabling part of the brain by surgically destroying it (usually by means of a high-voltage electrical current). A second method is to administer drugs that are suspected of having effects on certain neurotransmitters; upon drug administration, behavior can be observed. A third method is to electrically stimulate the brain; specifically, a microelectrode is inserted into the brain and a mild electrical current is used to activate the neurons in a particular site. (pp. 53-54)

3. There does appear to be a link between the amygdala and aggression, although other structures and processes are involved in this human behavior (and the amygdala has other functions). In particular, stimulation of the amygdala can result in feelings of anger, fear, and anxiety, and in violent actions. For example, your text discusses research by Kluver and Bucy (1937), two scientists who found that lesions in the amygdala reduced aggression in rhesus monkeys. Also, amygdala lesions have been used to treat people who were uncontrollably violent. In sum, the amygdala does appear to be intricately associated with aggressive responses. (p. 58)

4. There is a division of labor within the brain. For example, the left hemisphere receives information from the right side of the body, whereas the right hemisphere communicates with the left side of the body (p. 66). In addition, research on cerebral lateralization suggests that there are hemispheric differences in the connected brain; the left hemisphere controls verbal activities, whereas the right hemisphere plays a vital role in nonverbal activities (pp. 69-70). Also, split-brain research shows that when the corpus callosum is severed, and the two hemispheres are separated, they are no longer able to work as a team by sharing information gathered from each side of the body (information sent to the right hemisphere may not cross over to the left hemisphere, and vice versa). In such cases, it is possible to create a situation in which the two halves function in complete ignorance of each other – each with its own mind (pp. 66-67).

5. Plasticity refers to the capacity of the brain to change as a result of practice, use, and/or experience (p. 71). Although psychologists used to believe that the adult brain was fully developed and incapable of change, research now suggests that it is much more plastic or flexible than had been originally thought. For example, research on rats indicates that exposure to an "enriched" environment (with ladders, toys, and other stimuli that promote curiosity and stimulate physical and mental exploration) causes the development of thicker, heavier brain tissue with more dendrites and synapses. In fact, the type of stimulation may cause specific brain transformations; for example, rats who receive a lot of visual stimulation experience more visual cortex growth, whereas rats placed in an environment that requires balance and coordination form a more well-developed cerebellum. In addition, some research on humans now suggests that repeated stimulation of a particular body part (like the tapping of fingers) causes enhanced brain activity and maybe even dendritic growth (p. 72). Thus, it appears that the adult brain can be altered by environmental input.

CHAPTER 3

SENSATION AND PERCEPTION

CHAPTER OVERVIEW

Building upon the information presented in Chapter 2, this chapter examines the psychology of sensation and perception, two interrelated processes that enable us to acquire information about the world. First, the chapter focuses on sensation, the process whereby receptor cells in our sensory systems (e.g., ears) gather information from the environment (e.g., vibrating air molecules) and send that information to the brain for further processing. Specifically, the text examines measurement issues including absolute thresholds and difference thresholds, as well as signal-detection theory. Then, each sensory modality is discussed in turn (i.e., vision, hearing, smell, taste, touch, temperature, pain, coordination). The second part of the chapter explores perception, the process in which sensory information is selected, organized, and interpreted (e.g., we "hear" a sound and recognize it as part of a song we've heard before). In turn, the chapter examines the process of perceptual organization, the phenomena of perceptual constancies, and the factors involved in depth perception. The ways in which perception can be influenced by prior experience (called perceptual set) also are discussed, as are perceptual illusions. The chapter ends with a discussion of extrasensory perception, or perception in the absence of sensation.

CHAPTER OUTLINE

I. *What's Your Prediction* Does Culture Influence Depth Perception?

II. Measuring the Sensory Experience

    A. Absolute Thresholds

    B. Signal-Detection Theory

    C. Difference Thresholds

III. Sensation

    A. Vision
        1. Light

LEARNING OBJECTIVES

By the time you have read and reviewed this chapter, you should be able to:

1. Distinguish between the processes of sensation and perception and consider whether these processes are separate or linked (pp. 82-84).

2. Explain the concept of absolute thresholds and how these are derived (p. 84). Consider the relation between absolute thresholds and signal-detection theory (p. 85). Explain how difference thresholds are used to measure sensory capacities (pp. 85-86).

3. Discuss the visual sensory modality (pp. 87-95). Consider the properties of light waves (p. 87) and distinguish among the major structures of the human eye (pp. 88-91). Explain the processes of dark and light adaptation (p. 92).

4. Discuss how the eye, visual pathways, and the visual cortex are involved in visual sensation (pp. 91-93). Compare the trichromatic and opponent-process theories of color vision (pp. 93-95).

5. Discuss the auditory sensory modality (pp. 96-101). Consider the properties of sound waves (pp. 96-97). Examine the auditory system, including the structures of the ear and the auditory cortex (pp. 97-99).

6. Discuss the adaptive aspects of normal hearing, including auditory localization (p. 99). Consider types of hearing impairment (pp. 99-100) and the impact of environmental noise on hearing (pp. 100-101).

7. Examine the olfactory sensory modality and discuss the processes involved in the sensation of smell (pp. 102-103). Consider the factors (e.g., age, culture) that affect the sense of smell (pp. 102-103). Discuss whether pheromones affect human behavior (p. 103).

8. Consider the sensation of taste (pp. 103-104). Distinguish among types of taste and individual differences in taste sensitivity (p. 104).

9. Discuss the sensation of touch and what distinguishes this sensation from others (pp. 104-106). Distinguish between active and passive touch (p. 105). Consider the four basic types of sensation involved in touch (p. 105).

10. Examine the factors that affect the sensation of temperature (p. 106).

11. Consider the sensation of pain (pp. 106-107) and distinguish between gate-control theory and psychological control (pp. 106-107) as ways of decreasing pain awareness.

12. Consider the sensory systems involved in coordination (kinesthetic and vestibular) (pp. 107-108).

13. Discuss how sensory adaptation and selective attention enable the human sensory systems to respond to only particular types of information without confusion (p. 109).

14. Explain the process of perceptual organization (pp. 110-111). Define the concept of figure and ground (p. 110) and list and explain the five Gestalt "laws" of grouping (p. 111).

15. Define the concept of perceptual constancy (pp. 111-112). Discuss the factors that affect size constancy. (p. 112).

16. Consider the factors involved in depth perception; namely, binocular depth cues and monocular depth cues (pp. 112-114). Discuss whether depth perception is inborn or learned from experience (pp. 114-115).

17. Define the concept of perceptual set and examine how prior experiences and expectations can influence perception (pp. 115-117).

18. Provide examples of perceptual illusions and explain how such illusions may stem from overuse of "normal" perceptual rules (pp. 117-118).

19. Define extrasensory perception (p. 118). Examine the evidence both for and against ESP (pp. 119-120).

KEY TERMS

The following key terms and concepts are featured in this chapter and are important for you to know. Write out definitions of each term and check your answers with the definitions in the text on the pages listed.

Sensation (p. 82)
Transduction (p. 82)
Perception (p. 82)
Psychophysics (p. 84)
Absolute threshold (p. 84)
Signal-detection theory (p. 85)
Just noticeable difference (JND) (p. 86)
Weber's law (p. 86)
Cornea (p. 88)
Iris (p. 88)
Pupil (p. 89)
Lens (p. 89)
Accommodation (p. 89)
Retina (p. 89)
Rods (p. 89)
Cones (p. 89)
Fovea (p. 90)
Dark adaptation (p. 90)
Light adaptation (p. 90)
Optic nerve (p. 90)
Blind spot (p. 90)
Receptive field (p. 90)
Visual cortex (p. 91)
Feature detectors (p. 91)
Trichromatic theory (p. 93)
Afterimage (p. 94)
Opponent-process theory (p. 94)
Audition (p. 96)
White noise (p. 97)
Auditory localization (p. 99)
Conduction hearing loss (p. 99)
Sensorineural hearing loss (p. 100)
Olfactory system (p. 102)
Pheromones (p. 103)
Gustatory system (p. 103)
Taste buds (p. 104)
Gate-control theory (p. 107)
Kinesthetic system (p. 107)
Vestibular system (p. 108)

TEST QUESTIONS

Multiple-Choice Questions

Circle the correct choice for each question and compare your answers with those at the end of the Study Guide chapter.

1. The process in which raw physical energy is absorbed by sensory receptors is called
   a. sensation.
   b. perception.
   c. transduction.
   d. extrasensory perception.

2. The process in which energy that has been absorbed by sensory receptors is converted into neural signals that are then sent to the brain is called
   a. sensation.
   b. perception.
   c. transduction.
   d. extrasensory perception.

3. Joey has volunteered for a psychology experiment. His task is to gaze at a dark screen and indicate to the researcher whether or not he sees a point of light. The researcher is attempting to assess Joey's
   a. perceptual threshold.
   b. stimulus gate.
   c. absolute threshold.
   d. intensity point.

38

4. Psychophysics researchers define the _____ as the point at which a stimulus (like light or a sound) can be detected 50 percent of the time.
   a. JND
   b. difference threshold
   c. sensory adaptation
   d. absolute threshold

5. The difference threshold or just noticeable difference is defined as the smallest change in stimulation that people can detect _____ percent of the time.
   a. 25
   b. 50
   c. 75
   d. 100

6. Sofia is in her garden gathering flowers for a bouquet. She selects a bright red rose. What wavelengths are producing the color that she sees when she looks at the rose?
   a. short wavelengths
   b. medium wavelengths
   c. long wavelengths
   d. All of the above

7. Purity is to saturation as wavelength is to _____.
   a. color
   b. richness
   c. brightness
   d. strength

8. The _____ is a small, round hole in the center of the eye through which light passes.
   a. cornea
   b. iris
   c. pupil
   d. lens

9. Deb has brown eyes, Julie has hazel eyes, Pam has blue eyes, and Amy has green eyes. Which part of the eye causes these differences in eye color?
   a. cornea
   b. lens
   c. retina
   d. iris

10. The lens of the eye becomes rounder for focusing on nearby objects and flatter for focusing on distant objects. This process is known as
    a. retination.
    b. vision.
    c. light adaptation.
    d. accommodation.

11. Of the following children, whose pupils are the most dilated (the least contracted)?
    a. Paul, who is playing with a toy in complete darkness
    b. Jen, who is playing under the bed with a flashlight
    c. Matthew, who is playing outside under a shady tree
    d. Brian, who is playing outside in direct sunlight

12. Suppose that you came across a creature who could only see in black and white and whose vision was best at night. What would you guess about the retina of that creature?
    a. It contains only cones.
    b. It contains only rods.
    c. It contains a mixture of cones and rods.
    d. It contains neither cones nor rods.

13. Suppose that you came across another creature who could only see in color and whose vision was best during the day. What would you guess about the retina of that creature?
    a. It contains only cones.
    b. It contains only rods.
    c. It contains a mixture of cones and rods.
    d. It contains neither cones nor rods.

14. Which of the following "feature detectors" is present in the visual cortex?
    a. simple cells
    b. complex cells
    c. hypercomplex cells
    d. All of the above

15. The existence of _____ was a problem for the trichromatic theory of color vision.
    a. the color black
    b. the color white
    c. afterimages
    d. All of the above

16. Frequency is to pitch as amplitude is to _____.
    a. loudness
    b. timbre
    c. tonal quality
    d. white noise

17. The hammer, anvil, and stirrup are part of _____.
   a. the outer ear
   b. the middle ear
   c. the inner ear
   d. a jockey's riding gear

18. Hearing involves which of the following substances?
   a. air
   b. fluid
   c. hair
   d. All of the above

19. While walking to school, you think you hear someone calling your name. Without thinking, you turn to your right and glance across the street – and you see someone from your class waving at you. Your ability to turn in the direction of the sound of your name reflects
   a. sensory adaptation.
   b. cochlear ability.
   c. auditory localization.
   d. conduction.

20. Jim's little dog, Stinker, frequently urinates on the fence surrounding his yard. Other dogs now avoid the yard and the fence. Stinker's "marking" behavior and the subsequent avoidance behavior of the other dogs may reflect the activity of
   a. territoriality.
   b. pheromones.
   c. olfactory sensitivity.
   d. bad training.

21. Taste bud are most densely packed
   a. in the middle of the tongue
   b. on the tip of the tongue
   c. on the roof of the mouth
   d. at the back of the tongue

22. The flavor of a food substance is determined by
   a. taste.
   b. odor.
   c. temperature.
   d. All of the above

23. The largest organ in the human body is
   a. skin.
   b. the brain.
   c. the optic nerve.
   d. the heart.

24. Kate and Abby are playing with their pet parrot. The parrot rubs her head against Kate's arm, while Abby strokes the parrot's back. Kate is experiencing _____ touch, and Abby is experiencing _____ touch.
    a. passive; passive
    b. active; active
    c. passive; active
    d. active; passive

25. The sense of touch consists of which of the following sensations?
    a. pressure
    b. warmth
    c. pain
    d. All of the above

26. When you first bought your new watch, the band felt constricting and binding on your wrist. Now, you hardly notice that the watch is on your wrist. This change in your sensitivity is known as
    a. selective attention.
    b. sensory adaptation.
    c. synesthesia.
    d. sensory decline.

27. Mindi is taking an art class. Her assignment for this week is to paint a picture of a flower using individual "dots" of color. When she is finished, she asks you to evaluate her work. Although up close you can see each separate dot of paint, from a distance you perceive a unified picture of a beautiful flower. This example illustrates the Gestalt principle of
    a. proximity.
    b. continuity.
    c. closure.
    d. common fate.

28. A plane is descending from the sky for a landing. Joe, who has never seen a plane before, looks up in the sky and exclaims, "Look at that object! It's growing bigger and bigger!" Joe is demonstrating a lack of _____.
    a. size constancy
    b. figure-and-ground
    c. closure
    d. peripheral vision

29. Monocular depth cues enable us to do which of the following?
      a. perceive depth with one eye closed
      b. perceive depth at long distances
      c. "see" a three-dimensional image on an artist's canvas
      d. All of the above

30. Every night, an opossum comes into Mallory's yard and climbs up the tree outside her window. One night, her neighbor's cat climbs the tree. However, instead of recognizing the cat, Mallory glances out and "sees" the opossum. Mallory's error is the result of
      a. monocular cues.
      b. binocular depth cues.
      c. perceptual set.
      d. perceptual illusions.

True-False Questions

Indicate which of the following statements are true or false, and compare your answers with those at the end of the chapter.

T F 1. Current psychological theory suggests that sensation and perception are best conceptualized as separate and distinct processes.

T F 2. The opponent-process theory of color vision can explain color blindness.

T F 3. It is not currently possible to regenerate damaged auditory hair cells in humans.

T F 4. All smells have a chemical origin.

T F 5. The number of taste buds on the human tongue increases as we age.

T F 6. Pain is an objective, purely physical experience.

T F 7. As a general rule, information received by one sensory system does not cross over to another.

T F 8. The phrase "figure and ground" illustrates the first principle of perceptual organization.

T F 9. The ability to perceive depth is partially dependent on experience.

T F 10. Research provides compelling evidence for the existence of ESP.

Key Concepts Matching Exercises

Exercise #1: Vision

Match the key concepts on the left with the definitions on the right.

_____ 1. Color

_____ 2. Brightness

_____ 3. Saturation

_____ 4. Iris

_____ 5. Pupil

_____ 6. Cornea

_____ 7. Lens

_____ 8. Retina

_____ 9. Rod

_____ 10. Cone

_____ 11. Fovea

_____ 12. Optic nerve

a. light passes through this small hole in the eye

b. determined by a light wave's amplitude

c. clear window that bends and focuses light within the eye

d. light-sensitive receptor cell

e. clear structure that changes its shape to bring an image into focus

f. determined by a light wave's length

g. neural pathway that carries visual information to the brain

h. ring-shaped structure that provides eye color

i. center of the retina

j. determined by light waves' purity

k. color-sensitive receptor cell

l. cell layer lining the inside surface of the eyeball

Exercise #2: Hearing

Match the key concepts on the left with the definitions on the right.

_____ 1. Pitch

_____ 2. White noise

_____ 3. Loudness

_____ 4. Timbre

_____ 5. Outer ear

_____ 6. Oval window

_____ 7. Middle ear

_____ 8. Auditory localization

_____ 9. Conduction hearing loss

_____ 10. Sensorineural hearing loss

a. determined by the complexity of a sound wave

b. the ability to tell from which direction a sound comes

c. soft inner-ear membrane

d. the combination of all possible sound waves causes this phenomenon

e. caused by damage to the inner ear

f. animals can wiggle this structure to maximize sound reception

g. determined by the frequency of a sound wave

h. consists of the hammer, anvil, and stirrup

i. the amplitude of a sound wave causes this experience

j. caused by damage to the eardrum or middle ear

Essay Questions

Write out answers to the following brief essay questions. Compare your responses with the sample answers at the end of the Study Guide chapter.

1. Define both sensation and perception. Is it possible to have sensation without perception? What about perception without sensation? Answer both questions, using relevant examples cited in the text or from other sources.

2. What are pheromones and how do they affect behavior? Is there a human pheromone?

3. Last week, Teresa fell and broke her foot. Although her doctor prescribed painkillers, she does not want to use them. Knowing that you are taking an introductory psychology course, she turns to you for advice. What two psychological approaches or methods can you suggest that Teresa use in order to reduce her pain? Be specific.

4. What is a sensory "crossover?" Is this a common experience?

5. "Depth perception is an innate skill that all humans have at birth." Agree or disagree with this statement.

TEST SOLUTIONS

Multiple-Choice Solutions

1. a (p. 82)	11. a (p. 88)	21. b (p. 104)
2. c (p. 82)	12. b (p. 90)	22. d (p. 104)
3. c (p. 84)	13. a (p. 90)	23. a (p. 105)
4. d (p. 84)	14. d (pp. 92-93)	24. c (p. 105)
5. b (p. 86)	15. c (p. 94)	25. d (p. 105)
6. c (p. 87)	16. a (p. 97)	26. b (p. 109)
7. a (p. 87)	17. b (p. 98)	27. c (p. 111)
8. c (p. 88)	18. d (pp. 98-99)	28. a (p. 112)
9. d (p. 88)	19. c (p. 99)	29. d (pp. 113-114)
10. d (p. 88)	20. b (p. 103)	30. c (pp. 115-116)

True-False Solutions

1. F (p. 82)	6. F (p. 106)
2. T (p. 94)	7. T (p. 108)
3. F (p. 100)	8. T (p. 110)
4. T (p. 102)	9. T (p. 114)
5. F (p. 104)	10. F (pp. 119-120)

Key Concepts Matching Solutions

Exercise #1	Exercise #2
1. f	1. g
2. b	2. d
3. j	3. i
4. h	4. a
5. a	5. f
6. c	6. c
7. e	7. h
8. l	8. b
9. d	9. j
10. k	10. e
11. i	
12. g	

Essay Solutions

1. In the process of sensation, raw physical energy from the environment (e.g., light waves) is absorbed by our different sensory systems (e.g., receptor cells in the eyes) and then converted into neural signals that are sent to the brain. In perception, these neural signals are selected, organized, and interpreted (e.g., we "see" someone we know) (pp. 82-83). Therefore, these two processes are intricately linked.

    Yes, it is possible to have sensation without perception. For example, your text discusses the work of neurologist Oliver Sacks (1995), who presents a case study of a man (Virgil) who had been blind since he was a young child. When this man's sight was restored through surgical procedures, he could detect light, forms, movement, and color (he could sense), but he was unable to organize and interpret this information (no perception). He "saw," but didn't know what he saw! (pp. 83-84)

    There is an ongoing debate about whether it is possible to have perception without sensation (ESP). Some people (parapsychologists) believe that there are three types of extrasensory ability (telepathy, clairvoyance, and precognition). Some early evidence suggested that ESP may be possible (Rhine's work in the 1930s, discussed by your textbook author). However, much of the so-called "evidence" is anecdotal in nature; aside from these colorful stories, there is little truly compelling research evidence for ESP. (pp. 118-120)

2. Pheromones are chemicals secreted by animals to transmit signals (for example, a readiness to reproduce) to others (usually of the same species). Pheromones are implicated in the reproductive activity of bees, dogs, ants, and so on. However, there does not appear to be a human pheromone. Studies do indicate that humans can recognize other people by their body odor, but there is no hard evidence that we secrete a sexual attractant that influences the mating behavior of other humans. (p. 103)

3. The first approach you might tell Teresa about is the "gate-control" theory of pain. According to this theory, the nervous system can only process a limited number of sensory signals at one time. When the system is full, the spinal cord shuts a neural "gate" that blocks the passage of additional signals to the brain. The implication is that Teresa can stop or alleviate some of the pain caused by her broken foot by stimulating other areas of her body and creating competing sensations (she could, for example, have a deep massage, or rub her other foot very hard). The second approach is to block the pain from conscious awareness by practicing psychological control – basically, you could tell Teresa to "just not think about it." Although this can backfire (research suggests that the more we try to suppress a particular thought, the more readily it actually pops into our minds), Teresa could use distraction. She could focus on a specific aspect of the environment or of experience (for example, "What will I do tonight when I get home from school?") and thereby distract herself from the pain. (pp. 106-107)

4. Sensory crossovers happen when information that is received from one sensory system crosses over and is experienced by another sensory modality. For example, people with synesthesia ("joining the senses") might report that bright lights sound "loud"; thus, visual sensory information has crossed over and been experienced as auditory. This is, however, a rare condition. As a general rule, our sensory systems do not cross, and each system operates independently of the other. (p. 108)

5. Well, there is still a debate about this question! Research with infants using the "visual cliff" (a glass-covered table top with a shallow drop on one end and a steep "cliff" on the other) suggests that depth perception is evident at very young ages. Infants will crawl across the clear table top toward their parents at the shallow end, but they will not cross to the steep end; this suggests that they perceive the difference in depth. This suggests that depth perception might be innate; however, critics argue that perceptual learning begins at birth, and so by six months of age an infant has already had lots of perceptual practice. Cross-cultural research provides additional evidence that learning plays a large role in perception; your text presents a case study of a Pygmy who "saw" distant buffalo as insects when he was taken from his dense forest home to an open plain. His life experiences in the forest had been with objects densely packed together – objects that appeared small were small, in his experience. In sum, depth perception may be innate, but it is highly influenced by experience. (pp. 114-115)

CHAPTER 4

CONSCIOUSNESS

CHAPTER OVERVIEW

This chapter examines the state of awareness that psychologists call consciousness, or all the thoughts, sensations, and feelings of which we are aware at any given moment in time. First, the author examines three important attentional processes that influence consciousness: (1) Selective attention, a filtering process in which individuals selectively focus on one stimuli among many; (2) divided attention, the ability to apportion our consciousness among many competing stimuli; and (3) influence without awareness, or the process by which we are influenced by information outside the realm of our conscious awareness. The next part of the chapter explores sleep, including the sleep-wake cycle, the stages of sleep, and theories about the function or purpose of this particular state of consciousness. The content and interpretation of dreams are discussed, as are a variety of sleep disturbances (e.g., insomnia, hypersomnia, parasomnias). The third section of the chapter examines yet another state of consciousness, the one that is caused by a set of attention-focusing procedures called hypnosis. The author examines why the use of hypnosis has engendered controversy, describes the stages involved in hypnosis (i.e., induction and suggestion), and examines the myths and realities about hypnotic effects. Then, the chapter explores how human consciousness is affected by different types of drugs, including sedatives, stimulants, hallucinogens, and opiates. This chapter ends with an examination of whether or not people can exert control over the contents of conscious awareness.

CHAPTER OUTLINE

I. *What's Your Prediction* Do Subliminal Self-Help Tapes Work?

II. Attentional Processes

      A. Selective Attention

      B. Divided Attention

      C. Influence Without Awareness
          1. Mere exposure
          2. Priming

III. Sleep and Dreams

      A. The Sleep-Wake Cycle

V. Consciousness-Altering Drugs

    A. Sedatives
       1. Alcohol

    B. Stimulants

    C. Hallucinogens

    D. Opiates

VI. Consciousness and Control

VII. Thinking Like a Psychologist About Consciousness

LEARNING OBJECTIVES

By the time you have read and reviewed this chapter, you should be able to:

1. Define consciousness and describe the three processes that influence consciousness (pp. 126-127).

2. Explain the concept of selective attention and give examples of selective attention in different sensory modalities (pp. 127-128).

3. Describe the phenomenon of divided attention and discuss how the distinction between effortful and automatic processing explains this occurrence (pp. 128-129).

4. Consider whether it is possible to experience influence without consciousness (p. 130). Explain how mere exposure and priming may influence preferences and behavior below the threshold of conscious awareness (pp. 130-131).

5. Explain the difference between biological rhythms and circadian rhythms (pp. 131-132). Discuss the human sleep-wake cycle and whether it is determined by endogenous (internal) or environmental (outside patterns of lightness and darkness) forces (pp. 132-133).

6. Consider the relation between the sleep-wake cycle, night work (and other disruptions of the cycle), and health (pp. 133-135).

7. List the stages of sleep and identify the EEG patterns associated with each stage (pp. 135-137).

8. Distinguish between REM and NREM sleep (pp. 136-137).

9. Discuss the consequences of sleep deprivation (p. 138) and consider two theories about why sleep is a necessary function (pp. 138-139).

10. Explain the nature of dreams (e.g., is it adaptive to dream?) and discuss the content of dreams (pp. 139-140). Consider the factors that influence dream content (pp. 140-141).

11. Explain what is meant by lucid dreaming. (pp. 140-141).

12. Distinguish between the Freudian theory of dream interpretation and the activation-synthesis approach to understanding dreams (pp. 141-142).

13. List and describe the major sleep disturbances, including insomnia, hypersomnia, and parasomnias (pp. 142-147). Consider ways to overcome insomnia (pp. 144-145).

14. Define hypnosis and explain the stages involved in hypnosis (pp. 148-149). Discuss the concept of hypnotic responsiveness (pp. 149-150).

15. Discuss research on the effects of hypnosis (e.g., coercion, pain relief, posthypnotic suggestion, memory enhancement) (pp. 150-152).

16. Consider how eyewitness memory is affected by hypnosis (pp. 152-153).

17. Compare the special-process and social cognitive theories of hypnosis (pp. 153-155).

18. Explain how psychoactive drugs alter consciousness (p. 155). Explain the concepts of physical and psychological dependence (pp. 155-156).

19. Discuss the physical and psychological effects of sedatives, stimulants, hallucinogens, and · opiates (pp. 156-161).

20. Discuss whether it is possible to control consciousness, and consider methods used to focus attention (e.g., meditation) (pp. 161-162). Explain the concept of "ironic processes" in mental control (p. 162-163).

KEY TERMS

The following key terms and concepts are featured in this chapter and are important for you to know. Write out definitions of each term and check your answers with the definitions in the text on the pages listed.

Consciousness (p. 126)
Attention (p. 126)
Cocktail-party phenomenon (p. 127)
Selective attention (p. 127)

TEST QUESTIONS

Multiple-Choice Questions

Circle the correct choice for each question and compare your answers with those at the end of the Study Guide chapter.

1. Most psychologists define consciousness as the awareness of one's _____.
   a. sensations
   b. feelings
   c. thoughts
   d. All of the above

2. Jill is watching her roommate compete in a karate exhibition. Despite the large number of other competitors and the noisy spectators who keep walking in front of her seat, Jill is able to focus on her roommate. Her ability to do so illustrates
   a. selective attention.
   b. divided attention.
   c. unconscious motivation.
   d. subliminal perception.

3. People are able to exhibit divided attention among competing tasks when at least one of the tasks involves _____.
   a. effortful processing
   b. automatic processing
   c. the Stroop test
   d. selective awareness

4. Suppose someone asked you to remember where you went for vacation last year. According to Freud's view of levels of awareness, your memory came from
   a. conscious awareness.
   b. the preconscious.
   c. the unconscious.
   d. All of the above

5. Bernie doesn't remember seeing any of the pictures a researcher flashed on a screen in front of him. When the researcher asks him about the pictures, however, he indicates that he likes certain ones more than others. This could be an example of
   a. selective attention.
   b. priming.
   c. mere exposure.
   d. divided attention.

6. When a stimulus word is presented subliminally it can _____ responses to a subsequent target question.
   a. expose
   b. focus
   c. prime
   d. none of the above

7. The average person spends about _____ hours per day sleeping.
   a. 9
   b. 8
   c. 7
   d. 6

8. The average person spends about _____ minutes per day dreaming.
   a. 150
   b. 120
   c. 90
   d. 60

9. The changing of the seasons, the 28-day lunar cycle, the 24-hour day, and the 90-minute activity-rest cycle are examples of _____.
   a. circadian rhythms
   b. natural rhythms
   c. biological rhythms
   d. physiological clocks

10. Studies on people who live in environmentally controlled isolation chambers reveal that
    a. most people naturally settle into a short day.
    b. most people naturally settle into a longer sleep-wake cycle.
    c. most people have difficulty readjusting their biological clocks upon emergence.
    d. most people experience physical illness and mental strain.

11. Which one of the following individuals is most likely to experience jet lag?
    a. Sidney, who is flying east across two time zones
    b. Tammy, who is flying west across one time zone
    c. Cindy Sue, who is flying east within one time zone
    d. Bonnie, who is flying west within one time zone

12. Humans are _____ creatures.
    a. triurnal
    b. mono-urnal
    c. diurnal
    d. piurnal

13. While driving home late one night, you find yourself nodding off at the wheel for brief (two- to three-second) periods of time. These episodes are called
    a. micronaps.
    b. microsleeps.
    c. macrosleeps.
    d. cat naps.

14. As your classmate drones on endlessly about his summer plans, your breathing slows, your muscles relax, and you begin to feel drowsy. An EEG recording of your brain-wave activity will reveal:
    a. delta waves.
    b. zeta waves.
    c. alpha waves.
    d. beta waves.

15. _____ is to alert as delta is to deeply asleep.
    a. Theta
    b. Alpha
    c. Spindle
    d. Beta

16. Sleep spindles are typical of which stage of sleep?
    a. Stage 1
    b. Stage 2
    c. Stage 3
    d. REM sleep

17. Most dreams occur during _____ sleep.
    a. stage 1
    b. stage 2
    c. NREM
    d. REM

18. The circadian theory of sleep explains the need for sleep by focusing on which of the following?
    a. eating patterns
    b. predation patterns
    c. cross-species comparisons of sleep patterns
    d. All of the above

19. Who will spend the least amount of sleep time in REM sleep?
    a. Carlo, a premature newborn
    b. Ashleigh, a full-term newborn
    · c. Alex, a three-year-old
    d. Mackenzie, a ten-year-old

20. Dev is dreaming. Although asleep, he has the strange sensation of realizing that he is in a dream. His experience is known as
    a. circadian dreaming.
    b. nondreaming.
    c. lucid dreaming.
    d. hallucinatory dreaming.

21. A friend recounts a dream she once had in which she was taken to see the king and queen and given a knighthood for her bravery. Having just read your introductory psychology chapter on consciousness, you explain to her that she was "really" dreaming about her parents and their feelings about her decision to go to graduate school. Your analysis of this dream is based on _____.
    a. random guesswork
    b. activation-synthesis theory
    c. Freudian dream interpretation
    d. clinical neuropsychology

22. According to activation-synthesis theory, dreams originate in _____ and they represent _____.
    a. the brainstem; random neural impulses
    b. the unconscious; drive fulfillment
    c. the cortex; unconscious impulses
    d. manifest content; latent content

23. Insomnia may be a consequence of which of the following?
    a. stress
    b. beliefs about sleep requirements
    c. old age
    d. All of the above

24. Jacqueline has no problem falling asleep at night. However, once she is asleep, she stops breathing for brief periods of time until she awakens, choking and gasping for air. Jacqueline may have a condition called
    a. narcolepsy.
    b. sleep apnea.
    c. NREM sleep disruption.
    d. REM sleep behavior disorder.

25. Hypnosis results in which of the following?
    a. heightened suggestibility
    b. enhanced memory for actual events
    c. heightened sensitivity to pain
    d. All of the above

26. People who are highly susceptible to hypnosis tend to also be
    a. more obedient.
    b. highly dependent.
    c. imaginative.
    d. unskilled at memory tasks.

27. While jogging along his normal exercise path, Gil finds himself daydreaming about his plans for the future. Later, when Bobby asks him what he thought of the new trees that the city planted, he realizes that he didn't even notice them. What has Gil experienced?
    a. hallucination
    b. dissociation
    c. posthypnotic suggestion
    d. induction

28. Social-cognitive theories of hypnosis argue that the effects of hypnosis stem from
    a. dissociation.
    b. induction.
    c. special process.
    d. social influence.

29. Which of the following drugs is capable of altering consciousness?
    a. cocaine
    b. amphetamines
    c. LSD
    d. All of the above

30. Maggie has ingested heroin, Joel has had a few beers, RuthAnn has taken a dose of LSD, and Ed has snorted cocaine. Who will experience the most dramatic change in consciousness?
    a. Maggie
    b. Joel
    c. RuthAnn
    d. Ed

True-False Questions

Indicate which of the following statements are true or false, and compare your answers with those at the end of the chapter.

T F   1. It is not possible to divide attention between competing tasks.

T F   2. Current psychological theory suggests that subliminal messages have no effect on human behavior.

T F   3. For the mere exposure effect to occur, people must be aware of their prior exposures to a stimulus.

T F   4. It is possible to "prime" some aspects of human behavior.

T F   5. The circadian rhythm is determined solely by endogenous factors.

T F   6. Prolonged late-night activity results in diminished productivity and reaction time.

T F   7. There is little compelling evidence that humans need to sleep.

T F   8. The essential ingredient of hypnotic induction is a focusing of attention.

T F   9. You cannot be hypnotized against your will.

T F   10. Psychoactive drugs can become psychologically or physically addictive.

Key Concepts Matching Exercises

Exercise #1: Consciousness and Sleep

Match the key terms on the left with the definitions on the right.

_____ 1. Consciousness	a. 24-hour biological cycle
_____ 2. Selective attention	b. semiconscious dream state
_____ 3. Divided attention	c. sudden "attacks" of REM sleep
_____ 4. Circadian rhythm	d. the ability to focus on one stimulus and ignore others
_____ 5. REM sleep	e. the conscious or surface content of a dream
_____ 6. Lucid dreaming	f. the "deepest" sleep stage
_____ 7. Latent content	g. most dreams occur during this stage of sleep
_____ 8. Manifest content	h. cessation of breathing during sleep
_____ 9. Narcolepsy	i. what you are currently sensing, thinking, and feeling
_____ 10. Sleep apnea	j. the ability to distribute attention among different activities
_____ 11. Stage 4 sleep	k. the "hidden" meaning of a dream

Essay Questions

Write out answers to the following brief essay questions. Compare your responses with the sample answers at the end of the Study Guide chapter.

1. What is selective attention and how does it affect consciousness? Give an example of selective attention in two different sensory modalities.

2. Is the circadian rhythm of the human sleep-wake cycle controlled by endogenous factors alone? Consider evidence from isolation studies in your answer.

3. Why do humans sleep? Consider two theories about the purpose or function of sleep.

4. Discuss whether REM sleep is biologically adaptive. Consider three sources of evidence when constructing your answer.

5. Is hypnosis an "altered" state of consciousness? Compare the special-process and social-cognitive response to this question.

TEST SOLUTIONS

Multiple-Choice Solutions

1. d (p. 126)
2. a (p. 127)
3. b (pp. 128-129)
4. b (p. 130)
5. c (p. 130)
6. c (p. 130)
7. b (p. 131)
8. c (p. 131)
9. c (p. 131)
10. b (p. 132)

11. a (p. 133)
12. c (p. 133)
13. b (p. 134)
14. c (p. 136)
15. d (pp. 135-136)
16. b (p. 136)
17. d (p. 137)
18. d (pp. 138-139)
19. d (p. 139)
20. c (p. 140)

21. c (p. 141)
22. a (p. 142)
23. d (p. 144)
24. b (p. 146)
25. a (pp. 149-152)
26. c (p. 150)
27. b (p. 153)
28. d (pp. 154-155)
29. d (pp. 155-156)
30. c (pp. 159-166)

True-False Solutions

1. F (pp. 128-129)
2. F (p. 130)
3. F (p. 130)
4. T (p. 130)
5. F (p. 132)

6. T (p. 134)
7. F (pp. 138-139)
8. T (p. 149)
9. T (p. 149)
10. T (p.155)

Key Concepts Matching Solutions

Exercise #1

1. i
2. d
3. j
4. a
5. g
6. b
7. k
8. e
9. c
10. h
11. f

Essay Solutions

1. Selective attention is the process in which people are able to focus on a single stimulus and ignore other, competing stimuli. This affects the information that is included or excluded from consciousness; through this process, we become aware of one stimulus but then we lose conscious awareness of the other stimuli (p. 127).

   You could draw your examples from any sensory modality. For example, in the auditory modality (hearing), research indicates that people who are presented with two messages at the same time (this is called a dichotic listening task) are able to "shadow" one of the messages with great accuracy; however, they lose track of the other message. The same phenomenon may happen in the visual system. For instance, people who watch two videotapes, one superimposed on the other, are able to follow the action and events of one videotape but they become unable to focus on and remember the events of the other. (pp. 127-128)

2. No, the human sleep-wake cycle is not controlled solely by endogenous (internal) factors, although we do have a "timing device" in our brains in the form of the hypothalamus and the pineal gland; these structures take in information about light from the optic nerve and then work to either facilitate or retard feelings of sleepiness (pp. 132-133).

   Evidence from isolation studies suggests that the human sleep-wake cycle is at least partly determined by outside patterns of lightness and darkness. Your text presents the story of a woman who volunteered to live in a cave that was sealed off from any environmental cues (e.g., sunlight, outside noises, temperature changes, clocks). Over the course of her 131-day stay, her "day" had extended to 48 hours; she slept and woke up later and later. However, when re-exposed to sunlight, she readjusted her biological clock (p. 132).

3. There are two theories about why humans seem to need sleep. The first is restoration theory, which states that sleep is a time for the body to rest and repair or restore itself from the exertions of the day. This theory accounts for the feeling of rejuvenation most people feel after a night's sleep and is supported by research on sleep deprivation using animals (in which rats placed in stressful situations and deprived of sleep became ill and ultimately died) (p. 138). [Also recall the information in Chapter 2 (Behavioral Neuroscience) about how the autonomic nervous system regulates the internal body environment; when we are resting, our parasympathetic system is engaged in conserving energy and getting us ready for the next time we need to be active.]

   The second major theory of sleep is the circadian explanation, which focuses on the adaptive purpose of sleep. According to this theory, sleep is an evolved mechanism that enables us (and all other species) to conserve energy and minimize our exposure to predators. Humans sleep at night because such behavior is adaptive; our eyes are not equipped to see well in the dark, and so it makes evolutionary "sense" for us to be quiet and protected during times of darkness (pp. 138-139).

4. Most researchers now believe that REM sleep is biologically adaptive. There are three sources of evidence in support of this belief. First, there is evidence that suggests that REM sleep is necessary for brain maturation; that is, the brain is incredibly active during REM sleep, and REM sleep therefore may be a way for the brain to "test drive" itself. Indeed, infants (whose brains are still developing) spend more time in REM sleep than older children and adults, and premature infants spend even more time in REM sleep. Cross-species comparisons provide the second source of evidence for the biological benefits of REM sleep – all mammals and most birds experience REM sleep, which suggests that cognitive complexity and cortex development go hand in hand with REM sleep. Finally, when people are deprived of REM sleep one night, they experience a "rebound effect" by spending more time in REM sleep the next night (as if the brain is trying to make up for lost REM time). (p. 139)

5. Psychologists do not agree on the answer to this question. Special-process theorists argue that hypnosis is in fact a unique state of consciousness in which one part of the mind dissociates or operates independently of another. Theorists who follow this approach point to evidence from pain-tolerance studies in which participants immersed their hands in ice water and rated their level of pain. Those who were hypnotized to "feel no pain" reported less pain than non-hypnotized individuals. However, when they were told to press a key with their free hand if "some part" of them was in pain, they did so; this suggests that they experienced a division of consciousness, with one part feeling pain that the other part did not. (pp. 153-154)

   Social-cognitive theories argue that hypnosis does not result from a division of consciousness or an altered state of consciousness but rather from social influence processes. For example, it is possible that hypnosis effects are the result of a desire to comply with experimenter suggestion. Research indicates that the same pain tolerance effects outlined above can result simply from instilling sufficient motivation in participants. (pp. 154-155)

   At this point, both theories may explain the phenomenon – perhaps highly motivated people experience hypnosis as a dissociative state.

CHAPTER 5

LEARNING

CHAPTER OVERVIEW

This chapter explores the processes involved in three types of learning. The author begins by defining learning and examining the difference between learned behavior and instinctive behaviors (fixed action patterns). Next, the chapter examines a basic form of learning called classical conditioning. The fundamental principles of this type of learning (e.g., acquisition, extinction, generalization, and discrimination) are discussed, as are recent advances in classical conditioning theory. This foray into classical conditioning ends with an examination of the practical applications of this type of learning. The second part of Chapter 5 is devoted to operant conditioning; in turn, the law of effect, the basic principles of reinforcement and punishment, the impact of schedules of reinforcement on behavior, and the practical applications of operant conditioning are discussed. This section ends with an examination of recent developments in the arena of operant conditioning, including research on the ways in which biological predispositions constrain or interfere with the shaping of a new behavior, and the manner in which cognitive perspectives have been incorporated into operant conditioning theory. The third section of the chapter concerns observational learning. Classic studies in observational learning are presented, and the processes involved in this form of learning (attention, retention, reproduction, motivation) are discussed.

CHAPTER OUTLINE

I. *What's Your Prediction* Can People Learn Without Realizing It?

II. Classical Conditioning

    A. Pavlov's Discovery

    B. Basic Principles
        1. Acquisition
        2. Extinction
        3. Generalization
        4. Discrimination

    C. Pavlov's Legacy
        1. Theoretical advances
            a. Biological preparedness

2. Practical applications
    a. Conditioned fears
    b. Social attitudes and behavior

D. *Psychology and Health* Can the Immune System Be Classically Conditioned?

III. Operant Conditioning

  A. The Law of Effect

  B. The Principles of Reinforcement
    1. Shaping and extinction
    2. Schedules of reinforcement
      a. Fixed-interval (FI) schedule
      b. Variable-interval (VI) schedule
      c. Fixed-ratio (FR) schedule
      d. Variable-ratio (VR) schedule
    3. Punishment
    4. Stimulus control
    5. Self control

  C. Practical Applications of Operant Conditioning

  D. *How To* Condition Yourself to Break a Bad Habit

  E. New Developments in Operant Conditioning
    1. Biological constraints
    2. Cognitive perspectives
      a. Latent learning
      b. Locus of control
      c. Hidden costs of reward

IV. Observational Learning

  A. Studies of Modeling

  B. The Process of Modeling

V. Thinking Like a Psychologist About Learning

LEARNING OBJECTIVES

By the time you have read and reviewed this chapter, you should be able to:

1. Distinguish between learning and fixed action patterns (pp. 168-169). Define the process of habituation and give examples of this type of learning (p. 169).

2. Define association (p. 170). Outline the process of classical conditioning (pp. 181-172).

3. Discuss four basic principles of classical conditioning, including the acquisition and extinction of a classically conditioned response, and the process of stimulus generalization and discrimination (pp. 172-174).

4. Discuss how research on biological preparedness has changed the early Pavlovian stimulus-response approach to conditioning (pp. 175-176).

5. Consider practical applications of classical conditioning, including how this form of learning may be applied to understanding the development of negative (e.g., phobias) and positive preferences (p. 177), the formation of social attitudes (p. 179), aspects of social behavior (p. 180), and the immune system (p. 178).

6. Explain the types of behaviors that are influenced by operant as opposed to classical conditioning (pp. 180, 181).

7. Discuss how Thorndike's law of effect served as the basis for operant conditioning (p. 180).

8. Define operant conditioning and explain the difference between operant conditioning and classical conditioning (p. 181).

9. Distinguish between reinforcement and punishment and a positive and negative stimulus (pp. 181-182). Be able to provide examples of positive and negative reinforcement and punishment (pp. 181-182).

10. Explain the process of shaping and how it can be used to alter behavior (pp. 182-183).

11. Discuss how a shaped behavior can be extinguished (p. 183).

12. Identify four schedules of reinforcement and how each affects human behavior (pp. 183-185).

13. Discuss the consequences of punishment and the circumstances in which punishment is most effective (pp. 185-186).

14. Consider the process involved in stimulus control (pp. 186-187).

15. Discuss the concept of self-control and how it relates to operant conditioning (pp. 187-188).

16. Describe the practical applications of operant conditioning (pp. 188-189).

17. Consider how operant conditioning has been changed by research on biological predispositions and cognitive processes (pp. 189-194).

18. Define observational learning (p. 195).

19. Discuss how aggressive and cooperative behavior are learned via observation (pp. 195-196).

20. Discuss the four steps involved in observational learning (p. 196).

KEY TERMS

The following key terms and concepts are featured in this chapter and are important for you to know. Write out definitions of each term and check your answers with the definitions in the text on the pages listed.

Ethologists (p. 168)
Fixed action pattern (p. 168)
Learning (p. 169)
Habituation (p. 169)
Classical conditioning (p. 171)
Unconditioned response (UR) (p. 171)
Unconditioned stimulus (US) (p. 171)
Conditioned stimulus (CS) (p. 172)
Conditioned response (CR) (p. 172)
Acquisition (p. 172)
Extinction (p. 173)
Spontaneous recovery (p. 174)
Stimulus generalization (p. 174)
Discrimination (p. 174)
Law of effect (p. 180)
Skinner box (p. 181)
Operant conditioning (p. 181)
Reinforcement (p. 181)
Punishment (p. 182)
Shaping (p. 182)
Partial-reinforcement effect (p. 185)
Corporal punishment (p. 186)
Discriminative stimulus (p. 186)
Latent learning (p. 192)
Observational learning (p. 195)

TEST QUESTIONS

Multiple-Choice Questions

Circle the correct choice for each question and compare your answers with those at the end of the Study Guide chapter.

1. Which of the following is an example of instinctive behavior?
    a. a honeybee builds a hive out of wax
    b. a dog sits up and "speaks" for a treat
    c. a child learns how to ride a tricycle
    d. All of the above

2. The simplest form of learning is _____.
    a. classical conditioning
    b. habituation
    c. fixed action patterns
    d. instinct

3. Learned behavior is defined as
    a. relatively permanent.
    b. the result of experience.
    c. changed behavior.
    d. All of the above

4. Vicki recently adopted a baby crow who had fallen from her nest. When Vicki first tried to feed the bird, she backed away and crouched in the corner of the box. Now, however, the crow appears much calmer and she does not back away when Vicki approaches her. The baby crow has become _____.
    a. associated
    b. habituated
    c. weaned
    d. bored

5. You have volunteered for a psychology experiment. During the study, the experimenter presses a buzzer and then shoots a puff of air into your eyes, making you blink. After a few trials, you blink as soon as you hear the sound of the buzzer. In this example, the buzzer is the _____, and the puff of air is the _____.
    a. unconditioned stimulus; conditioned stimulus
    b. conditioned stimulus; unconditioned stimulus
    c. unconditioned response; conditioned response
    d. conditioned response; unconditioned response

6. In the previous question, your eyeblink in response to the puff of air is the _____ , and your eyeblink in response to the buzzer is the _____ .
   a. unconditioned stimulus; conditioned stimulus
   b. conditioned stimulus; unconditioned stimulus
   c. unconditioned response; conditioned response
   d. conditioned response; unconditioned response

7. The type of learning demonstrated in the previous question is _____ .
   a. habituation
   b. classical conditioning
   c. operant conditioning
   d. observational learning

8. Research on classical conditioning suggests that a response is acquired quickest when the conditioned stimulus (e.g., a buzzer) occurs _____ the unconditioned stimulus (e.g., puff of air, meat powder).
   a. immediately after
   b. at the same time as
   c. immediately before
   d. three hours before

9. Hank the cat always gets his dinner right after the clock chimes 5:00. As a result, he begins to salivate as soon as the clock chimes five times. His owner recently switched jobs and she is no longer able to feed him at 5:00; instead, she feeds him at 5:30. Now, Hank does not drool when the clock chimes at 5:00. Hank's response has been _____ .
   a. extinguished
   b. generalized
   c. discriminated
   d. acquired

10. Last year, little Heather got to play with her neighbor's poodle. Now, she smiles and approaches all dogs, even those that are larger than poodles. Heather's behavior illustrates
    a. acquisition.
    b. discrimination.
    c. generalization.
    d. extinction.

11. Your textbook discusses a research study in which rats were exposed to radiation right after they tasted sweetened water, saw a flash of light, and heard a loud clicking noise. These rats then became nauseous due to the radiation. What did they learn to avoid?
    a. the light
    b. the noise
    c. the water
    d. All of the above

12. Birds have extremely good eyesight; they respond more to the appearance of their food than to its taste or smell. If you were to place birds in the same situation as that outlined in Question 11 (i.e., have them taste sweetened water, see a flash of light, and hear a loud noise right before exposing them to radiation and making them nauseous), what would you expect them to avoid in the future? Think about this one!
    a. the light
    b. the noise
    c. the water
    d. All of the above

13. Research now suggests that people all over the world share many of the same fears. These results provide evidence that some learning is _____.
    a. behaviorally modified
    b. biologically programmed
    c. due to experience
    d. culture-specific

14. Research on the applications of classical conditioning suggests that humans can be conditioned to learn
    a. fears and preferences.
    b. negative attitudes.
    c. positive attitudes.
    d. All of the above

15. The "law of effect" suggests that
    a. behaviors that produce a negative outcome are more likely to recur.
    b. behaviors that produce a positive outcome are more likely to recur.
    c. behaviors that produce a neutral outcome are more likely to recur.
    d. All of the above

16. In what way does operant conditioning differ from classical conditioning?
    a. Operant conditioning involves reflexive behavior, whereas classical conditioning involves voluntary behavior.
    b. Operant conditioning produces positive outcomes, whereas classical conditioning produces negative outcomes.
    c. Operant conditioning happens quickly, whereas classical conditioning happens over time.
    d. None of the above

17. Reinforcement _____ the likelihood of a response; punishment _____ the likelihood of a response.
    a. increases; increases
    b. decreases; decreases
    c. increases; decreases
    d. decreases; increases

18. Parents praise their daughter every time she studies and brings home a good grade. Now, she spends even more time studying and is earning even higher grades. The praise she receives from her parents is a _____.
   a. positive punisher
   b. positive reinforcer
   c. negative punisher
   d. negative reinforcer

19. The same parents allow their daughter to skip her chores when she gets an "A" on a test or paper. The removal of chores serves as a _____.
   a. positive punisher
   b. positive reinforcer
   c. negative punisher
   d. negative reinforcer

20. Over time, you have trained your pet rat to crawl through a tunnel, run up a ladder, and walk across a bridge in order to receive a treat. The procedure you followed to train the rat is called
   a. shaping.
   b. approximate learning.
   c. reinforcement.
   d. bribery.

21. Both Keiko and Hiroko receive treats for doing their chores. Keiko knows that she will receive a treat if she does her chores five days in a row. However, Hiroko does not know exactly how often she will have to do her chores in order to get a treat. Keiko is on a _____ schedule, whereas Hiroko is on a _____ schedule.
   a. variable-ratio; fixed-ratio
   b. variable-interval; fixed-interval
   c. fixed-ratio; variable-ratio
   d. continuous; partial

22. A conditioned response is more resistant to extinction when it is reinforced on a(n) _____.
   a. partial basis
   b. continuous basis
   c. ratio schedule
   d. interval schedule

23. Punishment is most effective when it is
   a. immediate.
   b. consistent.
   c. inescapable.
   d. All of the above

24. What is one consequence associated with using punishment to decrease an unwanted behavior?
    a. Punished behavior is not necessarily extinguished.
    b. Punishment can result in negative emotions.
    c. Punishment does not replace the unwanted behavior with a more desired one.
    d. All of the above

25. A man has learned that his partner will engage in conversation and answer questions when the television is off but not when it is on. He now only converses with his partner when the television is off. The television is a
    a. positive reinforcer.
    b. discriminative stimulus.
    c. generalizer.
    d. punisher.

26. Principles of operant conditioning have been used successfully in which of the following settings?
    a. workplace
    b. health care system
    c. classroom
    d. All of the above

27. Try as you might, you cannot seem to teach your Vietnamese pot-bellied pig to pick up the morning paper and carry it to you. Wilbur has learned to approach the paper and touch it, but instead of picking it up he pushes it around on the ground with his snout. What does Wilbur's behavior demonstrate?
    a. willful disobedience
    b. classical conditioning
    c. instinctive drift
    d. operant conditioning

28. Reinforcement will strengthen behavior in a person who has a(n) _____ locus of control.
    a. internal
    b. external
    c. hidden
    d. latent

29. Which one of the following statements is accurate?
    a. Observational learning only occurs among primates.
    b. Complex new behaviors can be learned via observation.
    c. The ability to imitate a model's behavior develops during late childhood.
    d. Observational learning can account for aggressive but not helping behavior.

30. At the beach one day, you see a lifeguard administer CPR to another person. In order for you to learn this behavior by observation, you must
   a. remember the lifeguard's behavior.
   b. have the ability to administer CPR.
   c. be motivated to administer CPR.
   d. All of the above

True-False Questions

Indicate which of the following statements are true or false, and compare your answers with those at the end of the chapter.

T F   1. We may be biologically predisposed to learn some associations more easily than others.

T F   2. Attitudes and preferences cannot be classically conditioned.

T F   3. Classical conditioning provides the best explanation for the learning of simple reflexive behaviors.

T F   4. Continuously reinforced responses are the most difficult to extinguish.

T F   5. Inconsistent punishment is the most effective way to suppress an unwanted behavior.

T F   6. Biological predispositions may interfere with the shaping of a new behavior.

T F   7. Research on latent learning suggests that operant conditioning may occur without direct reinforcement.

T F   8. Perceptions, expectations, and beliefs appear to have no significant effect on the operant conditioning of a response.

T F   9. Observational learning of complex behavior may occur in many types of animals.

T F   10. Observational learning can occur in infants.

Key Concepts Matching Exercises

Exercise #1: Schedules of Reinforcement

Match each reinforcement schedule with its definition, example, and effect on behavior.

_____ 1. Continuous

_____ 2. Fixed-ratio

_____ 3. Variable-ratio

_____ 4. Fixed-interval

_____ 5. Variable-interval

a. timing of reinforcement is unpredictable from one period to the next

b. produces a fast, steplike response pattern

c. at this theater, customers receive a discount on movies every Tuesday night

d. reinforcement is administered after every response

e. customers receive a free car wash after every tenth car wash they purchase

f. this schedule is the least resistant to extinction

g. reinforcement occurs after a random number of responses

h. reinforcement is administered after a fixed number of responses

i. produces a slow, "scalloped" response pattern

j. every time the dog sits up and "begs," he gets a treat

k. in this store, discount coupons are mailed to customers depending on how much money they spent during the previous month; the amount needed to have been spent before receiving a coupon varies from month to month.

l. produces a slow but steady pattern of responses

m. reinforcement follows the first response made after a given amount of time has elapsed

n. produces a steady rate of responding and is very resistant to extinction

o. in this club, patrons receive free drink tokens at various random times during the week

Essay Questions

Write out answers to the following brief essay questions. Compare your responses with the sample answers at the end of the Study Guide chapter.

1. Use the example of conditioning of Little Albert to explain learning acquisition and stimulus generalization. How might Watson and Rayner have eliminated Little Albert's response?

2. A family friend is about to undergo chemotherapy treatment for a mild form of cancer. His doctors disagree over the best treatment program. Doctor A believes in the benefits of establishing and following a regular treatment routine. She has recommended that your friend arrive at the same hospital each week on the same day, and that chemotherapy occur at the same time in the same room and with the same technician. Doctor B prefers a more varied treatment regimen. She suggests that your friend receive the same dose of chemotherapy, but in different hospitals and with different technicians each week. Whose advice should your friend follow? Base your answer on recent research on classical conditioning and the immune system.

3. Andy's roommate never picks up her clothes. Andy has been taking an introductory psychology course, and as he is reading about operant conditioning he decides to use positive reinforcement to change his roommate's behavior. Define positive reinforcement and give an example of how Andy might use operant conditioning in this situation. (Hint: What must first happen for reinforcement to work?)

4. Becky's dog Abigail eats the legs off chairs. Becky is running out of usable chairs and she wants this behavior to stop. She is thinking of using punishment to change Abigail's behavior. Should she? Define punishment and discuss when it is most effective. Consider the possible consequences of punishment.

5. Outline and describe (using an example) the four steps involved in observational learning. In what way does operant conditioning play a role in observational learning?

TEST SOLUTIONS

Multiple-Choice Solutions

1. a (p. 168)
2. b (p. 169)
3. d (p. 169)
4. b (p. 169)
5. b (pp. 171-172)
6. c (pp. 171-172)
7. b (p. 171)
8. c (pp. 172-173)
9. a (p. 173)
10. c (p. 173)

11. c (p. 175)
12. a (pp. 175-176)
13. b (p. 176)
14. d (pp. 177, 179)
15. b (p. 180)
16. d (p. 181)
17. c (pp. 181-182)
18. b (p. 181)
19. d (p. 181)
20. a (pp. 182-183)

21. c (pp. 184-185)
22. a (p. 185)
23. d (p. 185)
24. d (p. 186)
25. b (p. 186)
26. d (pp. 188-189)
27. c (p. 191)
28. a (p. 192)
29. b (p. 195)
30. d (p. 196)

True-False Solutions

1. T (p. 176)
2. F (p. 179)
3. T (p. 180)
4. F (p. 185)
5. F (p. 185)

6. T (p. 191)
7. T (pp. 191-192)
8. F (p. 194)
9. T (p. 195)
10. T (p. 195)

Key Concepts Matching Solutions

Exercise #1

1. d, f, j
2. b, e, h
3. g, k, n
4. c, i, m
5. a, l, o

Essay Solutions

1. Acquisition is where a learned response (CR) is formed to a stimulus (CS) by presenting it paired with an Unconditioned Stimulus (UCS). Watson and Rayner taught an 11-month old boy, Little Albert, to fear white lab rats by making a loud crashing noise every time the boy reached for the animal. After only seven repetitions the animal terrified the boy. Little Albert's fear also generalized. Generalization is where the CR occurs in the presence of a stimulus that is similar to the CS. Little Albert showed a fear response not only to the lab rat, but also to a rabbit, a dog, a Santa Claus mask, and even a white fur coat. Watson and Rayner also did nothing to extinguish Little Albert's response because he was taken away before they had a chance to do so. This response could have been removed by continuing to present the white rat to Little Albert, but no longer pairing it

76

with the loud noise. If the rat were shown often enough without the noise, eventually it should no longer elicit the fear response. (pp. 172-174, 177)

2. Assuming that your friend receives the same quality of care and the same chemotherapy dose in both treatment programs, he or she should probably follow the advice of Doctor B (the varied program). Recent research suggests that classical conditioning processes can actually weaken the immune system, and this is something your friend cannot afford. For example, chemotherapy drugs (US) cause two responses – inhibition of new cancer cell growth and inhibition of immune cell growth (UR). It is possible that cues in the surrounding environment (like a particular treatment room or a particular technician who administers the chemotherapy) become associated with the chemotherapy drugs (US) and thus serve as powerful conditioned stimuli (CS). The consequence, of course, is that these environmental settings can actually result in the CR (immune cell inhibition). Thus, it would be best for your friend to undergo treatment in varied settings; this might prevent his or her immune system from "learning" to weaken in response to a particular situational cue. (p. 178)

3. Positive reinforcement involves presenting a stimulus in order to increase the likelihood of a particular response. There are a number of positive stimuli that might work in this situation. For example, Andy might smile and thank his roommate every time she engages in the desired behavior; alternately, he might loan his roommate a CD, or bake her cookies or type a paper for her. The problem with using positive reinforcement in this situation is that Andy can only reinforce a behavior that actually occurs – and we know that his roommate does not pick up her clothes. Thus, Andy must rely upon shaping, a process in which he will gradually guide his roommate toward the desired response by reinforcing responses that come closer and closer to it. For example, Andy could smile and thank his roommate (or give her food or whatever) every time she hangs her coat up, or every time she throws her clothing down in the general vicinity of the laundry basket or closet. After a while, Andy might only reinforce his roommate for leaving clothing three feet from the laundry basket/closet, then one foot from the basket/closet, and so on. (pp. 182-183)

4. Punishment is anything that decreases the likelihood of a behavior. It's a coin toss as to whether Becky should or should not use punishment to stop her dog's behavior. On the one hand, punishment that is strong, immediate, consistent, and inescapable does appear to suppress unwanted responses. However, punishment can have unwanted side effects. For example, punishment may temporarily inhibit a behavior but not extinguish that behavior. That is, Abigail may stop chewing on the chairs in Becky's presence, but continue to do so when Becky is not in the house (she may also stop her chewing behavior in Becky's house, but then destroy the chairs in other people's houses). In addition, punishment only teaches an individual what not to do; it does not teach the individual what to do. Abigail may learn not to chew chairs, but she will not learn which objects are acceptable to chew (like toys or bones). Third, punishment may backfire if the attention is rewarding – perhaps when Becky scolds her, Abigail gets the attention she wants. Finally, punishment may cause fear, anger, and aggressive responses – perhaps

Abigail will learn to fear Becky rather than learning not to chew, or perhaps she will bite Becky out of fear. In sum, it would be best if Becky used light punishment (immediate, consistent, etc.) along with positive reinforcement for desired behaviors. (pp. 185-186)

5. Observational learning involves four related steps. First, to learn by observation, we must pay attention to the model's behavior and to the consequences of that behavior. For example, Child A might see Child B help Child C go down a slide at the park, and then see Child B receive praise for her actions. Second, we must remember what we originally observed. In order for Child A to learn from the behavior of Child B, he or she must think about and remember that behavior and its consequences. Third, we must have the ability to actually reproduce the modeled behavior. Child A may attend to and remember Child B's helpful behavior, but physically be unable to climb a ladder and help another child down the slide. Fourth, we must be motivated to engage in the modeled behavior. Child A could be able physically to help another child go down a slide, but be too tired to help or already be involved in another, more interesting activity. (p. 196)

Operant conditioning plays a role in the last step of observational learning – motivation. Specifically, our motivation to engage in a modeled behavior is not only affected by the consequences we've seen the model receive (vicarious reinforcement and punishment), but also by our own direct personal experience with reinforcement and punishment. For example, if Child A has been reinforced in the past for helping other children on the swing set, he or she may be motivated to model a different form of helping behavior (i.e., helping others on the slide).

CHAPTER 6

MEMORY

CHAPTER OVERVIEW

This chapter explores the structures and processes of human memory from an information-processing perspective. The first structure that is examined is the sensory register, the initial step in the information-processing system. Both iconic and echoic memories are examined. The chapter then turns to the second information-processing step; namely, short-term or working memory. Your author explores the capacity and duration limits of short-term memory, as well as the functions of this active workspace. The final type of memory that is examined is long-term memory, an enduring storage area that can hold vast amounts of information. In this section of the chapter, the author explains the process involved in storing information in long-term memory (i.e., encoding), discusses the manner in which this information is stored (i.e., semantic coding, visual imagery), outlines the different types of long-term memories that can exist (i.e., procedural, declarative), and examines the neural bases of long-term memory. The process involved in retrieving long-term memories is discussed, and the techniques used to assess both explicit and implicit memories are presented. The section on long-term memory ends with a discussion of forgetting (why we forget and ways to prevent information from being lost from the system) and memory reconstruction (e.g., how we create false or illusory memories). The chapter concludes with a consideration of autobiographical memory, including the types of events or information that are best recalled.

CHAPTER OUTLINE

I. *What's Your Prediction* Can a Memory be Created?

II. An Information-Processing Model

III. The Sensory Register

    A. Iconic Memory

    B. Echoic Memory

IV. Short-Term Memory

    A. Capacity

    B. Duration

C. Functions of Short-Term Memory
    1. Working memory
    2. The serial-position effect

V. Long-Term Memory

  A. Encoding

  B. Storage
    1. Formats of long-term memory
    2. Contents of long-term memory
    3. Neural bases of long-term memory
      a. Where is the "engram"?
      b. The biochemistry of memory

  C. Retrieval
    1. Explicit memory
      a. Context-dependent memory
      b. State-dependent memory
    2. Implicit memory
      a. Implicit memory in amnesia patients
      b. Implicit memory in everyday life

  D. Forgetting
    1. The forgetting curve
    2. Why do people forget?
      a. Lack of encoding
      b. Decay
      c. Interference
      d. Repression

  E. *How To* Improve Your Memory

  F. Reconstruction
    1. The misinformation effect
    2. The creation of illusory memories

  G. *The Process of Discovery* Elizabeth F. Loftus

VI. Autobiographical Memory

  A. What Events Do People Remember?

VII. Thinking Like a Psychologist About Memory

LEARNING OBJECTIVES

By the time you have read and reviewed this chapter, you should be able to:

1. Define the concept of memory (p. 202) and explain the information-processing model of human memory (p. 203). Consider the parallel processing alternative to the information-processing model of memory (p. 204).

2. Discuss the sensory register (pp. 204-205). Distinguish between iconic and echoic memory (pp. 204-205). Explain the purpose of sensory memories (p. 205).

3. Explain the different types of encoding that can move information from sensory into short-term memory (p. 206).

4. Consider how attention limits the capacity of short-term memory (p. 206). Discuss the actual capacity of short-term memory and how chunking can add to the efficiency of short-term memory (pp. 206-208).

5. Discuss the duration of short-term memory (i.e., the length of time information can exist in short-term memory before it is lost) (pp. 208-209). Consider how maintenance rehearsal affects short-term memory (p. 209).

6. Explore the functions of short-term memory (pp. 209-211).

7. Define long-term memory (p. 211) and explain how information is transferred (encoded) into long-term memory (p. 212).

8. Discuss long-term memory storage, including its format (semantic versus visual; p. 213), content (procedural versus declarative; semantic networks; pp. 214-216), and neural bases (anatomical structures and biochemical processes; pp. 216-218).

9. Distinguish between explicit and implicit memories and consider the techniques to assess these types of memory (pp. 218-220).

10. Consider the factors that affect the retrieval of long-term explicit memories (i.e., encoding specificity, context, state of mind; pp. 221-222).

11. Consider implicit memory in amnesia patients (pp. 222-223), and explain the consequences of retention without awareness (i.e., eyewitness transference, unintentional plagiarism; pp. 224-225).

12. Explain the forgetting curve and what it demonstrates about memory failure (pp. 226-227).

13. Consider the four processes that can produce forgetting or memory failure: Encoding (lack of), decay, interference, and repression (pp. 227-229).

14. Define the concept of mnemonics and discuss eight techniques that we can use to increase our ability to retain information (pp. 230-231).

15. Consider the reconstructive nature of memory (pp. 232-236). Explain how schemas may distort memory (pp. 232-233). Define the misinformation effect (pp. 233-234). Examine evidence that misinformation may alter a witness's memories (p. 234).

16. Discuss the creation of illusory (false) memories and consider the differences, if any, between illusory and true recollections (pp. 234-236).

17. Define autobiographical memory (p. 236). Explain which aspects of our past we tend to remember (e.g., flashbulb memories; pp. 236-238).

KEY TERMS

The following key terms and concepts are featured in this chapter and are important for you to know. Write out definitions of each term and check your answers with the definitions in the text on the pages listed.

Memory (p. 202)
Information-processing model (p. 202)
Sensory memory (p. 202)
Short-term memory (p. 202)
Long-term memory (p. 202)
Iconic memory (p. 204)
Echoic memory (p. 205)
Chunking (p. 207)
Maintenance rehearsal (p. 209)
Working memory (p. 209)
Serial-position curve (p. 210)
Elaborative rehearsal (p. 212)
Procedural memory (p. 214)
Declarative memory (p. 214)
Semantic network (p. 215)
Hippocampus (p. 216)
Anterograde amnesia (p. 216)
Retrograde amnesia (p. 216)
Explicit memory (p. 219)
Implicit memory (p. 219)
Free recall (p. 219)
Recognition (p. 219)
Encoding specificity (p. 221)
Forgetting curve (p. 226)

TEST QUESTIONS

Multiple-Choice Questions

Circle the correct choice for each question and compare your answers with those at the end of the Study Guide chapter.

1. Magdalena is a cognitive psychologist. She is preparing to give an invited address at the American Psychological Association's annual conference. Most likely, her topic will be
   a. "Human Memory: The Faithful Workbench."
   b. "Human Memory: A Library Filled With Books."
   c. "Human Memory: The Extraordinary Computer."
   d. "Human Memory: A Busy Switchboard."

2. According to the information-processing model of human memory, a stimulus (for example, a sound) that registers on our senses will be remembered only if it
   a. catches our attention.
   b. is encoded in the brain.
   c. is retrieved for later use.
   d. All of the above

3. The process whereby information is received from the environment and transferred to storage sites in the brain is known as
   a. encoding.
   b. brain transfer.
   c. sensation.
   d. saving.

4. According to the information-processing model, memory works in a _____ fashion. According to the parallel-processing model, memory works in a(n) _____ fashion.
   a. linear; sequential
   b. passive; active
   c. sequential; simultaneous
   d. perpendicular; parallel

5. Lawrence is reading a chapter in his psychology text. As he reads, he recalls the sounds of the words themselves. This type of encoding is called
    a. semantic.
    b. visual.
    c. echoic.
    d. acoustic.

6. "The magical number seven, plus or minus two" refers to the capacity of which type of memory?
    a. sensory
    b. short-term
    c. long-term
    d. autobiographical

7. Chunking allows people to
    a. increase the capacity of short-term memory to 20 individual pieces of information.
    b. improve their powers of concentration.
    c. enhance the duration of information in short-term memory.
    d. None of the above

8. Upon meeting someone for the first time, Hildie silently repeats the person's name over and over to herself in order to really "learn" it. She is using _____ to encode this information.
    a. maintenance rehearsal
    b. working memory
    c. serial-positioning
    d. elaborative rehearsal

9. Short-term memory contains which of the following?
    a. central executive processor
    b. auditory storage-and-rehearsal system
    c. visual/spatial storage-and-rehearsal system
    d. All of the above

10. Roger's short-term memory system has an unlimited capacity. What is he likely to experience?
    a. increased intelligence
    b. constant distraction
    c. schizophrenia
    d. extreme emotional reactions

11. The term "working memory" refers to the fact that short-term memory
    a. is the hardest working of the memory systems.
    b. is a passive workplace where information is held.
    c. supplies the workforce that enables the human memory system to function.
    d. is an active mental workspace where information is processed.

12. Maintenance rehearsal can be used to maintain an item in short-term memory for how long?
    a. seven seconds
    b. five to nine seconds
    c. an indefinite period
    d. no time

13. Alejandro met a lot of new people at the dorm party last night, and he tried to memorize the names of each one. This morning, try as he might, he can only remember the names of the first few people he met. This illustrates
    a. the recency effect.
    b. the primacy effect.
    c. the serial-position effect.
    d. the short-term fallacy.

14. Jheri also met a lot of new people at the dorm party last night, but she can only remember the names of those she met toward the end of the evening. This illustrates
    a. the recency effect.
    b. the primacy effect.
    c. the serial-position effect.
    d. the short-term fallacy.

15. Four students are learning a list of words. Dee repeats the words over and over to herself; Ann counts the number of letters in each word; Heidi pronounces the words to see if they rhyme with her name; and Laura thinks about the meaning of each word and fits it into a sentence. Who will be most successful at transferring the words into long-term memory?
    a. Dee
    b. Ann
    c. Heidi
    d. Laura

16. _____ involves thinking about material that one wants to learn in a more meaningful way and associating it with other knowledge that is already stored in memory.
    a. Elaborative rehearsal
    b. Rote repetition
    c. Maintenance rehearsal
    d. Encoding rehearsal

17. Participants in a psychology study are asked to sit in front of a computer screen and look at ten trait words (for example, *shy, intelligent, friendly*). Participant A is asked to judge the length of each word. Participant B is asked to judge whether the words begin with a consonant or a vowel. Participant C is asked to judge whether the words rhyme with certain other words. Participant D is asked to judge whether the words are self-descriptive. Which participant will have the best recall?
    a. Participant A
    b. Participant B
    c. Participant C
    d. Participant D

18. Research indicates that long-term memory is better when
    a. information is processed at a "deep" level.
    b. information is "overlearned."
    c. information is learned over a period of time rather than all at once.
    d. All of the above

19. Our stored knowledge of learned habits and skills is called _____ memory.
    a. declarative
    b. episodic
    c. procedural
    d. semantic

20. Research suggests that the _____ is essential for the formation of new long-term memories.
    a. hypothalamus
    b. hippocampus
    c. frontal lobes
    d. temporal lobes

21. As part of a research project, Jenn attempted to learn a set of nonsense syllables. Which of the following would provide evidence that she in fact, did store the syllables in memory?
    a. She can recall the nonsense syllables when asked to do so by the experimenter.
    b. She can correctly select the original syllables out of a larger list of syllables.
    c. It takes her less time to relearn the same syllables.
    d. All of the above

22. Four people learn a list of words in a lecture hall. Later, each is taken to a specific location and asked to recall the original items. According to research on encoding specificity, who should have the best recall?
    a. the person who recalls the words in his or her own room
    b. the person who recalls the words in a different classroom
    c. the person who recalls the words in the same lecture hall
    d. the person who recalls the words outside under a tree

23. Lorelei was a participant in the study mentioned in Question 22. When she learned the list of words, she was in a particularly good mood. Research on state-dependent memory suggests that she will be able to recall the most words when she is
    a. in a particularly bad mood.
    b. in a particularly good mood.
    c. in a neutral mood.
    d. drunk.

24. People with _____ may show signs of long-term retention of information without awareness.
    a. schizophrenia
    b. alcoholism
    c. amnesia
    d. depression

25. Dean and some other students are brainstorming ideas for a class project. Later, when describing some of the ideas he himself generated, Dean "remembers" an idea that was actually generated by another student. This demonstrates
    a. unintentional plagiarism.
    b. eyewitness transfer.
    c. illusion of truth.
    d. blatant dishonesty.

26. An inability to recall information may be caused by which of the following?
    a. a failure to encode the information
    b. the passage of time
    c. interference by other information
    d. All of the above

27. Xena has arrived for a study session. The teaching assistant asks her to wait for the rest of the group in a small, cluttered "office." Almost immediately, however, she is taken to another room. When asked to remember the "office," which item(s) is she likely to recall seeing?
    a. a desk that was actually present
    b. books that were not actually present
    c. a television that was not actually present
    d. a and b

28. Research on autobiographical memory suggests that we are most likely to remember
    a. events from the distant past.
    b. events that represent "transitional firsts."
    c. routine events.
    d. events that happened before we were 3 or 4 years old.

29. When he was younger, Antonio received an outstanding citizen award for rescuing three people from a burning building. Although over 20 years have passed, his memory for that occasion is as vivid and detailed as if he is still standing on that platform, hearing the mayor speak his name, and seeing the crowd of cheering people. Antonio's memory would be described as a(n)
   a. amnesiac memory.
   b. egocentric memory.
   c. flashbulb memory.
   d. hindsight memory.

30. People's earliest memories are usually of events that took place
   a. shortly after birth
   b. between 1 and 2 years of age
   c. between the ages of 3 and 4
   d. after age 5

True-False Questions

Indicate which of the following statements are true or false, and compare your answers with those at the end of the chapter.

T F   1. Sensory memory stores all stimuli that register on the senses.

T F   2. With practice, the capacity of short-term memory can be expanded to hold an infinite number of items.

T F   3. Chunking allows us to make more efficient use of our short-term memory capacity.

T F   4. Short-term memory has a limited capacity but an unlimited duration.

T F   5. Maintenance rehearsal is one way to prevent information loss in working memory.

T F   6. The majority of modern memory researchers conceptualize short-term memory as a passive storage depot where information is held.

T F   7. Multiple mechanisms are needed to explain the serial-position curve.

T F   8. Long-term memory is better when the practice is spread over a long period of time than when it is crammed in all at once.

T F   9. All of memory is stored in the hippocampus.

T F   10. Memory without awareness occurs in all humans.

Key Concepts Matching Exercises

Exercise #1: Memory

Match the key terms on the left with the definitions on the right.

_____ 1. Sensory memory

_____ 2. Short-term memory

_____ 3. Long-term memory

_____ 4. Iconic memory

_____ 5. Echoic memory

_____ 6. Maintenance rehearsal

_____ 7. Elaborative rehearsal

_____ 8. Procedural memory

_____ 9. Declarative memory

_____ 10. Proactive interference

_____ 11. Retroactive interference

_____ 12. Mnemonics

_____ 13. Flashbulb memory

_____ 14. Childhood amnesia

a. "I can't remember my old phone number. I keep thinking of the new one."

b. "I remember it like it was yesterday, it's so clear and vivid in my mind."

c. "I learned to ski when I was five. I remember how excited I got when I first saw snow."

d. "This contains all of the information I've learned and all the memories I've formed."

e. "To really learn this material, I'll think about its meaning and how it relates to my own life."

f. "This records information from all of my sensory systems."

g. "I before E except after C," "30 days has September, April, June, and November."

h. "This is a brief memory for the sounds that I hear."

i. "I can't remember my new password. I keep thinking of the old one."

j. "When putting on skis, one must first insert the toe and heel of one foot."

k. "I can't remember anything from before I was 4 years old."

l. "This is my working memory."

m. "To learn this information, I'll just repeat it over and over again."

n. "This is a brief memory for the visual images that I see."

Essay Questions

Write out answers to the following brief essay questions. Compare your responses with the sample answers at the end of the Study Guide chapter.

1. The sensory memory system is capable of storing information for only a brief period of time. What is the point of forming memories that are lost almost immediately?

2. What is the serial-position effect? What explains this effect?

3. While walking to the university one day, Eric witnessed a man driving a car, run through a stop sign. Later that day, his friend Sandy asks him about the incident. Eric remembers the event, but he can't seem to recall the man's face or the color of the car. What four factors might explain Eric's memory failure?

4. Knowing that you are studying memory, a friend approaches you and asks for help in learning material for a big history exam. What techniques might you suggest that your friend follow or use in order to prevent forgetting the material?

5. According to your text "Memory is an active construction of the past. . ." Discuss the ways we reconstruct memories and how our schemas can sometimes lead to distortions. What is the misinformation effect?

TEST SOLUTIONS

Multiple-Choice Solutions

1. c (p. 203)
2. d (p. 203)
3. a (p. 203)
4. c (p. 204)
5. d (p. 206)
6. b (p. 206)
7. d (p. 207)
8. a (p. 209)
9. d (p. 209)
10. b (p. 209)

11. d (p. 209)
12. c (p. 209)
13. b (p. 210)
14. a (p. 210)
15. d (p. 213)
16. a (p. 212)
17. d (p. 212)
18. d (p. 212)
19. c (p. 214)
20. b (pp. 216-217)

21. d (pp. 219-220)
22. c (pp. 221-222)
23. b (p. 222)
24. c (pp. 222-223)
25. a (p. 224)
26. d (p. 227)
27. d (pp. 232-233)
28. b (p. 237)
29. c (pp. 237-238)
30. c (p. 238)

True-False Solutions

1. T (p. 203)
2. F (p. 207)
3. T (p. 207)
4. F (p. 208)
5. T (p. 209)

6. F (p. 209)
7. T (pp. 210-211)
8. T (p. 212)
9. F (p. 217)
10. T (p. 224)

Key Concepts Matching Solutions

Exercise #1

1. f
2. l
3. d
4. n
5. h
6. m
7. e
8. j
9. c
10. i
11. a
12. g
13. b
14. k

Essay Solutions

1. Although it might seem pointless to create sensory memories that fade almost immediately, such memories actually serve an incredibly important purpose. Specifically, these memories provide continuity between our perceptions of an event or stimulus. For example, the visual icon preserves an image of what we are seeing in memory, so that when we blink we do not experience a disturbance of that image. Without iconic memory, we would "see" the image as a series of disjointed snapshots rather than as a continuous, flowing film. The same purpose is provided by echoic and other forms of sensory memory (pp. 204-205).

2. The serial-position effect is the tendency for information that is presented earlier (this is called the primacy effect) and later (this is called the recency effect) to be better remembered than information that is presented in the middle. For example, if you received a list of words or met a series of people, you would probably remember the words or people first encountered (primacy) and those last encountered (recency); words and people sandwiched in the middle would not be recalled as well (p. 210).

   Different factors may be responsible for primacy and recency. For example, primacy appears to be a function of time spent rehearsing. That is, we begin rehearsing the first items, and can give them our undivided attention. However, we are less able to give attention (and devote time) to subsequent items. As noted by your author, the recency effect is harder to explain. It used to be thought that the last items were better remembered because they were still fresh in short-term storage when the recall test began; so, essentially, all the person had to do was "dump" whatever information was currently in short-term memory (and this information was the most recent, naturally). However, subsequent research indicates that this information may be better recalled not because it is still active in short-term memory, but because it is more distinctive (pp. 210-211).

3. Four factors might account for Eric's memory failure. The first two have to do with the possibility that the information is simply not in long-term memory. For example, it is possible that Eric saw the event, but he never actually encoded the information about the man's face and the car's color. Thus, he is unable to retrieve the information because it is not there and it never was there (this is called encoding failure). It is also possible that Eric did encode the information, but the memory for the man's face and car's color eroded with the passage of time (this is called decay). The next two factors that might explain Eric's memory failure have to do with the possibility that the memory exists but cannot be retrieved. For example, it is possible that other information is interfering with Eric's ability to retrieve the relevant details (perhaps he saw another person run a stop sign last week, and this old information is proactively interfering with the retrieval of the new information; or perhaps he saw another person run a stop sign right after the first man did, and this newer information is retroactively interfering with the first information). Finally, Eric may have encoded the information, but be unable to remember it due to a form of motivated forgetting called repression (perhaps the sight of

the man running the stop sign brought back traumatic memories of a traffic accident Eric once saw, and so he "forgets" what he's seen as a way of keeping that other painful memory out of awareness) (pp. 227-229).

4. There are several methods you could suggest to your friend to help him or her prevent forgetting the material. For example, your friend could increase his or her practice time; could think actively and deeply about the material; could organize and learn the material hierarchically; could make use of verbal mnemonics (e.g., rhymes, acronyms); could use the method of loci; could use the peg-word method; could attempt to reduce the likelihood of interference (e.g., by studying right before sleeping to minimize subsequent distracting information); and could attempt to reinstate the context in which learning occurred (i.e., make sure that the learning and testing context or situation are the same) (pp. 230-231).

5. Our memories are affected by what we know and believe about the world. We reconstruct memories according to our beliefs, wishes, needs and information received from outside sources (p. 232). The schemas we have can lead us to fill in missing pieces. For example, your book tells about a study where subjects were asked to wait in a small cluttered room that the experimenter called an "office." When they were later asked to recall what was in the room they remembered seeing books (consistent with our schema for offices) even though no books were present. The misinformation effect occurs when information we learn after observing an event becomes integrated into our memories. Loftus did a study where she found that subjects who viewed a slide show of a traffic accident were influenced by the wording of the questions researchers about the accident. They "remembered" seeing a stop sign when actually, a yield sign appeared in the slide show. (pp. 232-234).

CHAPTER 7

THOUGHT, LANGUAGE, AND INTELLIGENCE

CHAPTER OVERVIEW

This chapter examines the way people think and communicate, as well as the topic of intelligence. The first section focuses on thinking. Specifically, this section opens with an examination of the basic building blocks of thought, called concepts, and explores the ways in which we make use of these mental groupings when thinking and making judgments. Next, the mental activities or steps involved in problem solving are described (i.e., defining and representing the problem, generating and evaluating possible solutions), as are the biases or "blind spots" that prevent effective problem solving. The chapter then presents an overview of the rules of formal logic and a discussion of decision making in formal logic tasks, and ends with an examination of the biases that influence decision making and impede rational thought (e.g., heuristics, anchoring effects, overconfidence). The second section of the chapter focuses on language, beginning with a discussion of the characteristics of human language (i.e., semanticity, generativity, displacement). The chapter then moves into a consideration of whether the capacity for language is uniquely human or whether apes can also learn and use language for communication purposes. This section also explores the interrelationship between thought and language, starting with a discussion of the linguistic-relativity hypothesis (i.e., the notion that language influences thought). The third section of the chapter explores the topic of intelligence beginning with a consideration of the definitions of intelligence and the testing instruments that have been created to measure this construct. Your author discusses the essential "ingredients" of an intelligence test; that is, standardization, reliability, and validity. The question of bias in intelligence testing is addressed. Next is an overview of the major theorists who consider intelligence to be a general underlying mental capacity (e.g., Spearman). Then, multifactor models of intelligence are presented, including Gardner's "multiple intelligences" and Sternberg's "triarchic theory." Your author also explores the controversy surrounding the issue of whether intelligence is determined by genetics or the environment, and the empirical research that speaks to this issue. Group differences in IQ scores, and research concerning the origin of group differences, are discussed. This section ends with a consideration of gender differences in tests of specific abilities and the biological and environmental factors that might create the observed differences. The final part of the chapter explores the topic of education and how IQ-based teacher expectancies, stereotype vulnerability, and ability grouping may influence the educational process.

CHAPTER OUTLINE

I. *What's Your Prediction* Are People Smarter Today Than in the Past?

II. Concepts

III. Solving Problems

    A. Representing the Problem
        1. Mental images
        2. Mental models

    B. Generating Solutions
        1. Trial and error
        2. Algorithms and heuristics
        3. Insight

    C. "Blind Spots" in Problem Solving
        1. Representation failures
        2. Functional fixedness
        3. The confirmation bias

IV. Making Judgments

    A. The Rules of Formal Logic
        1. Syllogistic reasoning
        2. Conditional reasoning

    B. Biases in Judgment
        1. The representativeness heuristic
        2. The availability heuristic
        3. Anchoring effects
        4. Overconfidence

    C. *The Process of Discovery* Daniel Kahneman

    D. *How To* Improve Your Critical Thinking Skills

V. Language

    A. Communication in the Animal World

    B. Characteristics of Human Language
        1. Semanticity
        2. Generativity

C. Cultural Influences

D. Gender Differences

X. Education

    A. The Self-Fulfilling Prophecy
        1. Teacher expectancies
        2. Stereotype threat

XI. Thinking Like a Psychologist About Thought, Language, and Intelligence

LEARNING OBJECTIVES

By the time you have read and reviewed this chapter, you should be able to:

1. Define the term "concept" and explain how concepts are stored in memory (p. 245). Explain the relation between a concept and a prototype (p. 245). Discuss how prototypes affect judgment and decision-making processes (pp. 245-246).

2. List and describe the mental activities involved in the process of problem solving (p. 246).

3. Explain the different ways in which a problem may be represented mentally (i.e., words and concepts, mental images, mental models). Define mental images and mental models and explain how these representations affect problem solving (pp. 247-248).

4. List and describe the four basic problem-solving processes that we can use to generate solutions (pp. 248-252).

5. Discuss the "blind spots" that compromise problem solving (i.e., representation failures, functional fixedness, confirmation bias) (pp. 252-253).

6. Describe the ways in which people solve logical problems (p. 254).

7. Define the representativeness heuristic and explain how it affects judgment and decision making (p. 255).

8. Define the availability heuristic and examine the consequences this heuristic can have on judgment and decision making (pp. 255-257).

9. Explain the anchoring effect and consider how this phenomenon may bias problem solving (pp. 257-259).

10. Discuss the overconfidence effect (p. 259).

11. Define critical thinking and summarize the steps involved in critical thinking (p. 258).

12. Examine animal communication and compare it with human communication (pp. 259-260).

13. Describe and provide examples of the characteristics of human language, including semanticity (p. 261), generativity (p. 262), and displacement (p. 262).

14. Consider the developmental sequence of language acquisition (pp. 263-264) and define the concepts of babbling and telegraphic speech. Discuss whether nature (e.g., learning) or nurture (e.g., "universal grammar") propels language development (p. 264).

15. Explore the relationship between thought and language (pp. 266-268). In particular, explain the linguistic-relativity hypothesis (pp. 266-267). Consider how cultural differences in the use of words might enable researchers to evaluate this hypothesis (pp. 267-268).

16. Define the concept of intelligence (p. 269).

17. Compare different testing instruments used to measure intelligence, including the Stanford-Binet, Wechsler tests, and group tests (pp. 270-272).

18. Explain the concept of mental age and compare this concept to that of intelligence quotient (IQ) (p. 270). Discuss why the notion of IQ is useful for children but less so for adults (pp. 270-271).

19. Consider whether intelligence tests are "accurate" (pp. 272-274). Explain the measurement concepts of standardization, reliability, and validity (pp. 273-274).

20. Discuss whether intelligence tests are culturally biased (p. 274). Explain the concept of a "culture-fair" test (p. 274).

21. Define the concept of "g," or general intelligence (p. 275).

22. Contrast Spearman's notion of general intelligence with the theories of Thurstone, Gardner, and Sternberg (pp. 275-280).

23. Define the concept of multiple intelligences (p. 276). Discuss the converging lines of evidence that Gardner used to support this theory (p. 277). Contrast the seven major types of intelligence proposed by Gardner's theory (pp. 277-278).

24. Explain Sternberg's triarchic theory of intelligence (pp. 278-280). List and define the three types of intelligence proposed by this theory (pp. 278-280).

25. Summarize the research on the relative influence of genetics and environment on intelligence (pp. 281-282).

26. Explain the purpose of Head Start programs and how successful they are (pp. 283-284).

27. Consider racial and cultural differences in IQ score and research that has examined the origin of those differences (pp. 284-285).

28. Discuss gender differences in total IQ scores and in tests of specific abilities (i.e., verbal, mathematical, spatial) (p. 286).

29. Describe the phenomenon of the self-fulfilling prophecy (p. 288). Explain how IQ-based teacher expectancies can affect educational attainment in the classroom (p. 288).

30. Describe how stereotype threat (vulnerability) can contribute to a self-fulfilling prophecy (p. 289).

KEY TERMS

The following key terms and concepts are featured in this chapter and are important for you to know. Write out definitions of each term and check your answers with the definitions in the text on the pages listed.

Concept (p. 245)
Prototype (p. 245)
Image (p. 247)
Mental models (p. 247)
Trial and error (p. 248)
Algorithm (p. 248)
Heuristics (p. 248)
Means-end analysis (p. 249)
Analogy (p. 249)
Insight (p. 251)
Functional fixedness (p. 253)
Confirmation bias (p. 253)
Syllogism (p. 254)
Representativeness heuristic (p. 254)
Availability heuristic (p. 254)
Anchoring effect (p. 256)
Critical thinking (p. 258)
Language (p. 259)
Semanticity (p. 261)
Phonemes (p. 261)
Morphemes (p. 261)

TEST QUESTIONS

Multiple-Choice Questions

Circle the correct choice for each question and compare your answers with those at the end of the Study Guide chapter.

1. _____ are mental groupings of people, places, ideas, or objects that share common properties.
   a. Classifications
   b. Concepts
   c. Protoconcepts
   d. Mental models

2. Research suggests that a robin is the "birdiest" or most bird-like bird; that is, it is the prototype of the concept *bird*. What does this mean?
   a. A robin is perceived to be a more typical example of the concept *bird* than other members of the concept.
   b. A robin has more of the concept's characteristic or defining features than other members of the concept.
   c. A robin will be more easily recognized as a member of the concept *bird* than other members of the concept.
   d. All of the above

3. As part of a class demonstration, Val and other students are shown a slide of a tilted container filled with water. Val, along with many of his classmates, assumes that the water surface is tilted in the same way as the container – when, in fact, the water surface remains horizontal to the ground. This error may be due to the use of _____.
   a. mental models
   b. intuition
   c. prototypes
   d. formal logic

4. The simplest (and sometimes least efficient) problem-solving strategy that humans can make use of is called
   a. proto-logic.
   b. algorithms.
   c. trial and error.
   d. heuristics.

5. Jon and Linda enjoy word games, puzzles, and anagrams. Both are attempting to solve the following anagram: E H T E T. Jon tries all possible combinations by systematically varying the letters in each position. Linda tries the most familiar letter combinations (for example, she realizes that TH is a common combination in the English language). Both arrive at the solution (TEETH). Jon used a(n) _____, whereas Linda used a(n)

   _____.
   a. concept; prototype
   b. algorithm; heuristic
   c. means-end analysis; analogy
   d. insight; mental model

6. One important general heuristic involves breaking a larger problem (for example, writing a paper) into a series of smaller sub-goals (for example, obtaining references, which in turn means getting a library card). This heuristic is known as _____.
   a. analogy heuristic
   b. algorithm solution
   c. means-end analysis
   d. intuitive physics

7. Connor is using tacks to hang posters on the wall of his dorm room. He has only one more small poster to hang, but when he reaches for a tack, he discovers that the box is empty. He really wants to hang all the posters now, so he decides to use a fork to attach the poster to the wall. Connor's use of the fork demonstrates the absence of _____.
   a. mental sets
   b. functional fixedness
   c. representation failure
   d. reasoning

8. As a class demonstration, Dr. Allbright tells her students the following story: "There is a group composed of 20 classics professors and 80 truck drivers. In that group, I randomly select a conservative man named Harold who enjoys reading poetry and is shy, quiet, and thin. Is Harold a truck driver or a classics professor?" Most of the students in her class guess that Harold is a classics professor. Are they right?
   a. Yes, Harold resembles the typical classics professor.
   b. Yes, the probability is higher that a randomly selected man would be a classics professor than a truck driver.
   c. No, Harold resembles neither the typical classics professor nor the typical truck driver.
   d. No, they have ignored the base rate information given in the first sentence.

9. As noted by your textbook, people have a tendency to overestimate the likelihood of death by shark attack. This overestimation may be caused by
   a. the availability heuristic.
   b. the representativeness heuristic.
   c. anchoring.
   d. framing.

10. The ability to solve problems and make decisions through a careful evaluation of the evidence is known as
    a. formal logic.
    b. syllogistic reasoning.
    c. linguistic relativity.
    d. critical thinking.

11. Nick and Nora are in the process of insuring their valuable art collection. They need to evaluate the claims made by various insurance companies. What is the first critical thinking step they should follow?
    a. identify the assumptions that each company is making in its argument
    b. try to imagine alternative claims and arguments
    c. avoid being heavily influenced by big words and jargon
    d. adopt an attitude of healthy skepticism

12. All languages share three universal properties. What are they?
    a. semanticity
    b. generativity
    c. displacement
    d. All of the above

13. The basic sounds of a language are
    a. semantics.
    b. phonemes.
    c. morphemes.
    d. syllables.

14. The fact that the sentence you are reading at this very moment is unique (i.e., has never been written before) demonstrates which property of language?
    a. generativity
    b. semantics
    c. displacement
    d. syntax

15. The rules of grammar that govern how words can be arranged in a sentence are known as
    a. phonemes.
    b. language.
    c. deep structure.
    d. syntax.

16. The linguistic-relativity hypothesis states that language _____.
    a. is caused by thought
    b. influences thought
    c. is a product of higher thinking processes
    d. and thought influence each other

17. Most psychologists view the construct of intelligence as
    a. expertise on a particular academic subject.
    b. the capacity to learn from experience and adapt to one's environment.
    c. the ability to attain a high grade point average.
    d. professional success in one's chosen field.

18. The first psychologist to devise a "mental test" to measure intelligence was _____.
    a. Charles Darwin
    b. Alfred Binet
    c. Francis Galton
    d. Theopile Simon

19. The original intelligence test devised by Binet and Simon was developed in order to
    a. identify children needing special academic assistance.
    b. select men who were suited for military duty.
    c. predict worker productivity.
    d. determine the age at which children would reach their maximum academic potential.

20. The average eight-year-old child has a mental age of _____.
    a. 100
    b. 1
    c. 8
    d. 80

21. Suppose you were to take the Wechsler Adult Intelligence Scale (WAIS). What scores
    would you receive?
    a. a verbal score
    b. a nonverbal performance score
    c. an overall score
    d. All of the above

22. All intelligence tests should be _____.
    a. reliable
    b. valid
    c. standardized
    d. All of the above

23. Dr. O'Malley has developed a new intelligence test. She administers her test to a group of
    200 college students in early September and again in November, and then compares the
    two sets of test scores. Dr. O'Malley is assessing the _____ of her test.
    a. criterion validity
    b. standardization
    c. test-retest reliability
    d. split-half reliability

24. Which of the following statements about research on group differences in IQ scores is
    accurate?
    a. Test scores can be influenced by a person's racial and/or cultural background.
    b. Group differences are found on "culture-fair" test items.
    c. Test scores predict academic performance within a given culture, regardless of the
       race of the students.
    d. All of the above

25. According to Gardner's theory of intelligence, which of the following reflect "intelligent" behavior?
    a. the ability to play an instrument
    b. the ability to run at high speeds and/or over great distances
    c. the ability to design a building
    d. All of the above

26. Jenna can perform rapid-fire mental arithmetic and spends much of her time solving puzzles and equations. However, she is extremely awkward around other people and has a reputation for "always saying or doing the wrong thing at the wrong time." Gardner would say that Jenna has a high amount of _____ intelligence and a low amount of _____ intelligence.
    a. intrapersonal; relational
    b. logical-mathematical; interpersonal
    c. spatial; linguistic
    d. general; specific

27. Analytic intelligence is to "school smarts" as _____ intelligence is to "street smarts."
    a. social
    b. interpersonal
    c. practical
    d. creative

28. Studies designed to examine the relative influence of genetics and environment on intelligence generally find that
    a. identical (monozygotic) twins are more similar in their IQ scores than are fraternal twins.
    b. biological siblings raised together are less similar in IQ scores than biological siblings raised apart.
    c. children's IQ scores resemble the scores of their adoptive parents more than they do the scores of their biological parents.
    d. All of the above

29. Research indicates that
    a. about 50 percent of our IQ is inherited.
    b. heredity accounts for about 60-75 percent of the population variation in intelligence.
    c. the environment plays little to no role in intelligence.
    d. All of the above

30. Which of the following environmental factors might influence intelligence?
    a. family configuration
    b. amount of time spent in school
    c. prenatal care
    d. All of the above

True-False Questions

Indicate which of the following statements are true or false, and compare your answers with those at the end of the chapter.

T F 1. People may rely on prototypes when making decisions.

T F 2. People consistently underestimate the accuracy of their predictions.

T F 3. Morphemes are the basic sounds, or building blocks, of spoken language.

T F 4. Today, most psychologists agree that language influences the way we think.

T F 5. Mental age increases at the same rate as chronological age.

T F 6. The WAIS is the most widely used IQ test for adults.

T F 7. A valid test measures what it is supposed to measure.

T F 8. IQ test scores are highly predictive of professional (nonacademic) success.

T F 9. Research provides evidence for both a general intelligence and specific abilities.

T F 10. Most experts agree that intelligence is influenced by genetic factors.

Key Concepts Matching Exercises

Exercise #1: Thought

Match the key terms on the left with the definitions on the right.

_____ 1. Concept

_____ 2. Prototype

_____ 3. Mental model

_____ 4. Trial and error

_____ 5. Algorithm

_____ 6. Heuristic

_____ 7. Insight

_____ 8. Mental set

a. a systematic problem-solving strategy that is guaranteed to produce a solution

b. "I'll just keep plugging away and trying new combinations until I figure out the solution."

c. all your knowledge about the group of objects called "dogs"

d. intuitive theory about the way things work

e. "I'll just use the same strategy that worked last time."

f. the "doggiest" or most dog-like dog

g. "Experts are usually right."

h. "Eureka! I figured it out! The solution just came to me out of nowhere!"

Exercise #2: Testing Concepts

Match the concepts on the left with the examples or definitions on the right.

_____ 1. Standardization

_____ 2. Test-retest reliability

_____ 3. Split-half reliability

_____ 4. Content validity

_____ 5. Criterion validity

a. when scores from one test session are correlated with scores from a second test session

b. when the content of the test items reflects what the test is supposed to measure

c. enables psychologists to compare a person's score to existing norms

d. when the test scores accurately predict a particular outcome

e. when scores on one version of a test are correlated with scores on a second version

Essay Questions

Write out answers to the following brief essay questions. Compare your responses with the sample answers at the end of the Study Guide chapter.

1. What is trial and error? Explain this problem-solving strategy, using a specific example from your own experience. What are the consequences (positive and negative) of using trial and error?

2. Your friend Stan is working on a creative writing project. Unfortunately, he cannot figure out how to put the idea he has for a particular paragraph into words. He's rewritten this paragraph several times, and is becoming increasingly frustrated. "If I could just have the insight into how to set this down into words!" he exclaims. Define the notion of insight, and explain to Stan what he might do to increase his chances of experiencing insight.

3. List and define the "blind spots" that can prevent effective problem-solving.

4. Are IQ tests culturally biased or not? Consider both sides of the issue in your answer.

5. Do males and females differ in their specific abilities? Discuss the research on sex differences. What differences are there?

TEST SOLUTIONS

Multiple-Choice Solutions

1. b (p. 245)
2. d (p. 245)
3. a (p. 247)
4. c (p. 248)
5. b (p. 248)
6. c (p. 249)
7. b (p. 253)
8. d (p. 255)
9. a (p. 255)
10. d (p. 258)

11. d (p. 258)
12. d (p. 261)
13. b (p. 261)
14. a (p. 262)
15. d (p. 262)
16. b (p. 266)
17. b (p. 269)
18. c (p. 269)
19. a (p. 270)
20. c (p. 270)

21. d (p. 271)
22. d (p. 273)
23. c (p. 273)
24. d (p. 274)
25. d (pp. 276-278)
26. b (pp. 277-278)
27. c (p. 280)
28. a (pp. 281-282)
29. b (p. 282)
30. d (pp. 282-283)

True-False Solutions

1. T (p. 245)
2. F (p. 259)
3. F (p. 261)
4. T (p. 267)
5. F (p. 270)

6. T (p. 271)
7. T (p. 273)
8. F (p. 274)
9. T (p. 276)
10. T (p. 281)

Key Concepts Matching Solutions

Exercise #1

1. c
2. f
3. d
4. b
5. a
6. g
7. h
8. e

Exercise #2

1. c
2. a
3. e
4. b
5. d

Essay Solutions

1. Trial and error is the simplest problem-solving strategy, and it involves a "hit or miss" approach to a problem. Essentially, one would try a hodgepodge of potential solutions to a problem, in no particular order, and hope that one of these was correct. Any example from your own experience would be fine. For instance, I sometimes get an "error" message on the screen of my computer when running the SPSS/DOS statistical package. Often, I just go back to my command file and "tinker" with the commands; I might remove a comma, add a period, and so on. Then I try to rerun the analysis. I do this until

the system accepts my command and runs the analysis completely (or I get too tired and frustrated and put it aside!). There are both positive and negative consequences to employing trial and error as your strategy. On the positive side, it's a simple strategy and it's often effective. However, on the negative side, it may not be the most efficient strategy. For example, it often takes a long time and sometimes fails completely. (p. 248)

2. Insight is a problem-solving process in which the solution to a problem comes to mind all of a sudden, without conscious awareness. People who experience insight often do not realize that the solution is coming and cannot describe what they were thinking about at the time; it's almost as if the solution suddenly is just there. You might tell Stan that insight seems to be more likely when people do the following things: (1) They switch from one strategy to another (so maybe instead of writing things down, he could talk out loud for a while); (2) they reframe the problem (perhaps Stan should focus on the one basic point he wants to make, rather than the whole paragraph); (3) they remove a mental block (this is harder, maybe he could just free associate and write words and phrases down, instead of trying to create complete, entire sentences in a specified order); (4) they identify an analogy from prior experience; and (5) they take a break (walk away from) the problem (you might suggest that Stan go for a walk and stop consciously thinking about the problem). (pp. 251-252)

3. Your text discusses three "blind spots" that can prevent effective problem solving. First, there is something called representation failure; this is defined as incorrectly understanding or conceptualizing (representing) the problem. Functional fixedness may also prevent effective problem solving (this is the tendency to only think of objects in terms of their usual functions). Finally, the confirmation bias (the tendency to only look for evidence that confirms our existing beliefs) and belief perseverance (the tendency to maintain our initial beliefs even in the face of disconfirming evidence) may impede problem solving. (pp. 252-253)

4. As noted by your textbook author, there is evidence for both sides of the debate. Specifically, there is evidence for bias in that the question content of IQ tests does appear to favor the cultural and educational experiences of the dominant culture (in the United States, that culture is the white middle class). For example, to answer the question "Who was Thomas Jefferson?" one needs to have an understanding of American (as opposed to another country's) cultural heritage. In addition, a person's own cultural/racial/ethnic background can guide his or her perception of the testing situation itself and affect his or her scores. (p. 274)

On the other side of the debate, there is evidence that group differences are found even on test items that are considered to be "culture-fair," which suggests that the differences are not due solely to a lack of knowledge of the dominant culture. In addition, intelligence and aptitude tests are valid predictors of academic performance within a particular culture; individuals who obtain lower scores, irrespective of their race/ethnicity, in fact do not do as well academically as those who obtain higher scores. (p. 274)

110

5. Researchers have examined gender differences in three different areas; namely, verbal abilities, mathematical abilities, and spatial abilities. To date, the research indicates that (1) on verbal tests, girls tend to outperform boys (but the gender gap is decreasing); (2) on mathematical tests, girls outperform boys in grade school, but boys and men outperform girls and women in later grades and college; (3) on spatial tests, males tend to outperform females, and this is the most robust sex difference. (p. 286)

CHAPTER 8

NATURE AND NURTURE

CHAPTER OVERVIEW

This chapter focuses on the broad topic of nature and nurture, exploring the role that biological and environmental factors play in a variety of human behaviors. The chapter first considers genes (segments of DNA that are the biological units of heredity). How genetic material is transmitted from parent to offspring is considered, as is research on the human genome. In addition, how genes "work" is explored, with an emphasis on both direct effects of genes on phenotypic characteristics (e.g., blood type) and indirect effects on behavior dispositions (e.g., personality). The second part of the chapter focuses on evolution. This section begins with a consideration of Darwin's theory of natural selection. The core principles of natural selection are presented, and the process of adaptation by natural selection is explained. The field of evolutionary psychology is introduced, and evolutionary perspectives on various human behaviors (including aggression and helping behavior) are evaluated. The third part of the chapter presents the nature and nurture debate, beginning with a discussion of the methods available to researchers interested in teasing apart the relative contributions of genetic and environmental influences (i.e., the twin-study method and adoption studies). The chapter then presents the results of research that has been conducted using these methods and considers the way in which human behavior and development are influenced by an interplay or interaction between genetic and environmental forces. The final section of the chapter examines the nature and nurture debate in the context of two specific areas: Gender and sexual orientation. The way in which men and women differ in terms of biology, sexuality, aggressive behavior, and cognitive abilities is examined, and biological and environmental explanations for these differences are presented. Sexual orientation is then considered, including estimates about the prevalence of homosexuality and research exploring the origins of homosexuality.

CHAPTER OUTLINE

I. *What's Your Prediction* Nature or Nurture?

II. Genes

    A. What Genes Are and How They Work

    B. Genetic Building Blocks
       1. The Human Genome Project

    C. How Genes Affect Behavior

III. Evolution
    A. Natural Selection
        1. The process of natural selection
        2. The genetics of natural selection

    B. Evolutionary Psychology
        1. Evolutionary perspectives on human behavior
        2. Adapted, but to what?

IV. The Nature-Nurture Debates

    A. The Pursuit of Heritability

    B. Genetic Influences

    C. *Psychology and Medicine* The Debate About Cloning

    D. Environmental Influences

    E. *The Process of Discovery* Robert Plomin

    F. The Interplay of Nature and Nurture

V. The Nature and Nurture Of …

    A. Gender: A Great Divide?
        1. *How* are men and women different?
           a. Sexuality
           b. Physical aggression
           c. Cognitive abilities
        2. *Why* are men and women different?
           a. Biological perspectives
           b. Environmental perspectives
        3. A biosocial theory of sex differences
        4. Putting sex differences in perspective

    B. Sexual Orientation
        1. The numbers game
        2. Origins of homosexuality

VI. Thinking Like a Psychologist About Nature and Nurture

LEARNING OBJECTIVES

By the time you have read and reviewed this chapter, you should be able to:

1. Explain what genes are and explain the relationship among cells, chromosomes, deoxyribonucleic acid (DNA), and genes (pp. 297-298). Describe the two essential tasks that genes perform (p. 298).

2. Explain the genetic events involved in conception (pp. 298-299).

3. Describe the goals and major findings of the Human Genome Project (pp. 299-300). Explore why these findings met with a mixed reaction from the public and scientific communities (p. 300).

4. Consider whether genes predetermine and control human development. Discuss the association between genes and physical characteristics, diseases, thoughts, feelings, and behavior. Distinguish between a genotype and a phenotype (pp. 300-301).

5. Describe the principle of natural selection and identify the five core principles of natural selection (p. 302).

6. Define the concept of adaptation and discuss whether the process of natural selection occurs slowly over many successive generations or rapidly (p. 303). Explain how natural selection works at the genetic level (pp. 303-304).

7. Consider how natural selection "builds" behavioral adaptations as well as physical adaptations (pp. 304-305). Discuss how aggressive behavior and altruistic or helping behavior can serve an adaptive purpose (pp. 305-306).

8. Explain the concept of inclusive fitness and consider how it accounts for altruistic behavior that diminishes personal fitness (p. 306). Define kinship selection theory and explain how it accounts for the tendency to help individuals who are biologically related to us (p. 306). Consider how the notion of reciprocal altruism explains the tendency to help strangers (p. 306).

9. Explore the ways in which the ancestral environment (i.e., the environment in which our human forebears evolved) differed from the contemporary environment in which we live today (pp. 307-308). How do these differences allow us to understand the prevalence of certain maladaptive behaviors that contemporary humans display (e.g., overconsumption of fatty foods)?

10. Explain the nature-nurture debate (p. 309). Compare the strict biological (nature) position with the strict environmental (nurture) position (p. 309). Consider how psychologists today typically feel about the strict nature vs. nurture division (p. 309).

11. Explain how the field of behavioral genetics interprets the nature-nurture debate (i.e., what behavioral geneticists consider the "real" questions of interest to be; p. 309). Identify the two logically possible ways to examine the relative contribution of nature and nurture (p. 309).

12. Compare family studies, twin studies, and adoption studies and explain how each one has been used to examine the influence of biological and environmental influences on human behavior (pp. 309-310).

13. Define the concept of heritability (p. 310) and discuss what twin studies have shown about the heritability of various physical and psychological characteristics (pp. 310-311).

14. Consider what twin studies have demonstrated about the impact of the environment on human development (pp. 313, 315). Explain the difference between shared and nonshared environments (p. 313).

15. Consider the interplay between nature and nurture (i.e., how genetic and environmental factors influence each other) and explain bioecological model of development (p. 315).

16. Consider the ways in which men and women differ in terms of physical development, sexual attitudes and behavior, physical aggression, and cognitive abilities (pp. 316-318).

17. Compare the biological (pp. 318-319) and environmental (pp. 319-322) perspective on sex differences.

18. Explain how male-female differences may be linked to levels of the hormones testosterone and estrogen (pp. 318-319). Discuss the correlation between testosterone levels and aggressive behavior in animals and humans, and the relationship between testosterone and cognitive skills in humans (p. 319).

19. Discuss how environmental and social factors may explain the differences that are commonly observed between men and women (pp. 319-322). Define the concepts of gender role and gender schema, and explain how gender roles, gender schemas, and gender stereotypes are shaped by social and cultural forces (pp. 320-321). Consider how gender schemas and male and female stereotypes influence perception and behavior (pp. 320-321).

20. Describe the biosocial theory of sex differences and explain how differences between men and women may arise from an interaction between biological and social factors (pp. 322-323). Consider the numerous ways in which men and women are similar (pp. 323-324).

21. Define sexual orientation and consider the prevalence (p. 324) and the biological and social origins (pp. 325-327) of homosexuality. Explain why the origins of homosexuality are considered complex (p. 326).

KEY TERMS

The following key terms and concepts are featured in this chapter and are important for you to know. Write out definitions of each term and check your answers with the definitions in the text on the pages listed.

Genetics (p. 296)
Chromosomes (p. 296)
Deoxyribonucleic acid (DNA) (p. 297)
Genes (p. 297)
Human genome (p. 299)
Genotype (p. 300)
Phenotype (p. 300)
Natural selection (p. 302)
Adaptations (p. 303)
Mutations (p. 303)
Evolutionary psychology (p. 304)
Inclusive fitness (p. 306)
Kinship selection theory (p. 306)
Reciprocal altruism (p. 306)
Nature-nurture debate (p. 308)
Family studies (p. 308)
Heritability (p. 310)
Twin-study method (p. 310)
Adoption studies (p. 310)
Gender roles (p. 320)
Gender schemas (p. 320)
Sexual orientation (p. 325)

TEST QUESTIONS

Multiple-Choice Questions

Circle the correct choice for each question and compare your answers with those at the end of the Study Guide chapter.

1. The biological units of heredity are called
   a. cells.
   b. nuclei.
   c. molecules.
   d. genes.

2. Nucleus is to chromosome as _____ is to genes.
    a. molecule
    b. DNA
    c. cell
    d. protein

3. The results of the Human Genome Project indicate that
    a. all people are essentially the same genetically.
    b. humans have very few genes in common with mice and other mammals.
    c. it is impossible to sequence the human genome.
    d. All of the above

4. Scientists have determined that there is a <u>direct</u> link between genes and _____.
    a. social attitudes
    b. personality traits
    c. blood type
    d. aggressive behavior

5. Natural selection requires that the individual members of a species must
    a. be genetically identical.
    b. be equally suited to the demands of the environment.
    c. have the same chance of survival and reproduction.
    d. None of the above

6. Consider the following four groups. Society A consists of a colony of clones, each of whom is genetically identical. Society B consists of a group of males. Society C consists of a group of males and females who have just experienced a sudden drought. Society D consists of a group of males and females who live in an artificial environment that never changes. Which society is the most likely to experience evolution by natural selection?
    a. Society A
    b. Society B
    c. Society C
    d. Society D

7. Which one of the following statements best characterizes the process of natural selection?
    a. Natural selection sculpts adaptations out of mutations.
    b. Natural selection consciously designs "better" organisms.
    c. Natural selection works by a process of planning and foresight.
    d. Natural selection spontaneously creates new variations within a species.

8. According to the textbook, the evolutionary "bottom line" is
    a. how quickly a species can mutate.
    b. the propagation of genes.
    c. how long individuals survive.
    d. the number of species that exist on earth.

117

9. The subfield of psychology that uses the principles of natural selection and evolution to understand human social behavior is known as _____.
    a. social psychology
    b. social biology
    c. biological psychology
    d. evolutionary psychology

10. Which of the following social "facts" provides evidence for the evolutionary perspective on human behavior?
    a. There are multiple cross-cultural differences in how children are raised.
    b. Most nonhuman animals exhibit fixed action patterns.
    c. There are numerous cross-cultural similarities in food preferences and phobias.
    d. People do not exhibit fixed action patterns the many other organisms do.

11. One day a fire breaks out in the building where Dan lives. According to the principles of kinship selection theory, who is Dan most likely to help?
    a. his best friend Bob
    b. his new neighbor
    c. his daughter
    d. his uncle

12. The concept of reciprocal altruism helps to explain why people sometimes provide help or assistance to
    a. complete strangers.
    b. distant relatives.
    c. offspring.
    d. family members.

13. Dr. Nature is a behavioral geneticist interested in aggressive behavior in children. Which of the following research topics might reflect her orientation?
    a. peer influences on aggression
    b. genetic predispositions toward aggression
    c. aggressive behavior as a function of exposure to violent television
    d. cultural forces and aggression

14. Dr. Nurture works in the same department as Dr. Nature. He has just written a book. What might his book be titled?
    a. "Violent Television: Creating Aggressive Kids"
    b. "The Violence Gene: Making Aggressive Kids"
    c. "Aggression: Does it Run in the Family?"
    d. "Twin Studies of Aggressive Behavior"

15. A researcher is interested in the genetic basis for shyness. She compares the shyness scores of a group of children with the scores of their siblings, parents, aunts and uncles, and grandparents. What kind of research study is this?
    a. twin study
    b. behavior genetics experiment
    c. selective breeding study
    d. family study

16. The percentage of variation in a trait (like shyness) that is due to genetic factors is known as
    a. relatedness
    b. inheritance
    c. heritability
    d. monozygocity

17. In one of the twin studies mentioned in your text, the heritability estimates for personality characteristics averaged about 48 percent. This means that
    a. genetics control about 48 percent of human personality.
    b. about 48 percent of our personality is determined by our genetic makeup.
    c. personality in twins is caused by genetic factors.
    d. genetic factors account for about 48 percent of the variation in personality seen in that group of twins.

18. Twin studies and adoption studies have demonstrated that genetic factors are involved in which of the following aspects of human behavior?
    a. alcoholism
    b. intelligence
    c. aggressiveness
    d. All of the above

19. Which of the following research findings provides the strongest support for the pro-nurture position?
    a. Biological siblings who grow up in the same home are often different from each other.
    b. Twins raised apart are almost as similar to each other as those living together.
    c. Biological relatives resemble each other on personality traits.
    d. When raised together, monozygotic twins are more similar than dyzygotic twins.

20. Sophia and Lauren are sisters. They have the same parents, attend the same school, and vacation at the same summer camp. They each have a different best friend, and Sophia is in charge of the indoor chores whereas Lauren takes care of the outside chores. Aspects of their __shared__ environment are _____; their __nonshared__ environment includes _____.
    a. parents, school, and chores; best friend and vacation
    b. best friend and chores; parents, school, and vacation
    c. parents, school, and vacation; best friend and chores
    d. best friend; parents

21. The bioecological model of development suggests that
    a. genetic predispositions determine personality.
    b. inherited traits cause us to develop in a particular direction.
    c. genetic predispositions and life experiences interact to influence development.
    d. life experiences determine development.

22. The fact that children who are malnourished do not grow up to be as tall as they could be provides evidence for the _____ model of human development.
    a. biogenetic
    b. bioecological
    c. life experiences
    d. sociobiological

23. Research generally reveals a relationship between testosterone and
    a. sexual desire and interest.
    b. boldness and courageousness.
    c. aggressive behavior.
    d. All of the above

24. Gender roles can be communicated and taught by
    a. parents.
    b. peers.
    c. teachers.
    d. All of the above

25. Socially oriented researchers believe that the differences in mathematics ability for boy and girls might occur because
    a. girls receive less support from teachers.
    b. parents believe that girls are generally weak at math and see them as less competent.
    c. parents set lower expectations for their daughters.
    d. All of the above.

26. In which of these occupations is there a higher proportion of men then women?
    a. child-care worker
    b. bartender
    c. college instructor
    d. grade-school teacher

27. A person's preference for a sexual partner of a particular sex is known as
    a. partner preference.
    b. sexual orientation.
    c. sexual motivation.
    d. sexual response.

28. Research on homosexuality suggests that it is caused by
    a. a disturbed family environment.
    b. excessive attachment to the same-sex parent.
    c. the onset of puberty at an early age.
    d. None of the above

29. Research conducted by LeVay (e.g., 1993) on the brains of homosexual and heterosexual individuals indicates that
    a. sexual orientation is associated with the size of a hypothalamic nucleus.
    b. the hypothalamus causes sexual orientation.
    c. there is a gene that determines sexual orientation.
    d. AIDS may cause homosexuality.

30. The concept of erotic plasticity refers to the tendency to
    a. change sexual practices and preferences during one's lifetime.
    b. become sexually aroused by items made of plastic.
    c. develop a sense of sexual identity by adolescence.
    d. engage in gender-nonconforming behavior during childhood.

True-False Questions

Indicate which of the following statements are true or false, and compare your answers with those at the end of the chapter.

T F   1. All humans have certain genes in common.

T F   2. Genetically, people tend to cluster into five groups which correspond to the major geographical areas of the world.

T F   3. Most behavioral dispositions appear to be influenced by one single gene.

T F   4. It is impossible for evolution to occur in a rapid and observable manner.

T F   5. From an evolutionary perspective, the primary purpose of any organism is the propagation of genes.

T F   6. People do not exhibit fixed action patterns the way many other organisms do.

T F   7. Evolutionary psychology cannot explain the tendency for humans to help friends, acquaintances, and other nonrelated individuals.

T F   8. In general, researchers now agree that genetic and environmental influences are not entirely independent.

T F 9. Gender schemas do not begin to develop until boys and girls reach puberty.

T F 10. Cross-cultural research suggests that many stereotypes about men and women are universal.

Key Concepts Matching Exercises

Exercise #1: Genes

Match the key terms on the left with the definitions on the right.

_____ 1. Genes

_____ 2. Chromosomes

_____ 3. Proteins

_____ 4. Human genome

_____ 5. Nucleotide

_____ 6. Nucleus

_____ 7. Genotype

_____ 8. Phenotype

a. this structure is found inside every human cell except red blood cells

b. this is the genetic blueprint for a complete human being

c. this is an individual's observable physical and psychological properties

d. the DNA sequence that each individual inherits from his or her biological parents

e. these structures are considered the "building blocks of life"

f. these are tiny rodlike structures that contain deoxyribonucleic acid

g. stringy self-replicating molecules that constitute the biological units of heredity

h. this is a base or subunit of DNA

Exercise #2: Evolution

Match the key terms on the left with the definitions on the right.

_____ 1. Adaptations

_____ 2. Mutations

_____ 3. Inclusive fitness

_____ 4. Kinship selection theory

_____ 5. Reciprocal altruism

a. these are random gene copying errors

b. theory used to explain the tendency for us to help our biological relatives

c. inherited advantageous physical or psychological traits

d. explains the tendency for us to help strangers, acquaintances, and nonrelatives

e. the idea that an organism's genetic material is preserved through its own offspring and the offspring of genetic relatives

Exercise #3: Nature and Nurture

Match the key terms on the left with the items on the right.

_____ 1. Heritability

_____ 2. Twin study

_____ 3. Adoption study

_____ 4. Bioecological model

a. "Do adopted children resemble more closely their biological parents or their adoptive parents on various traits?"

b. "I believe that infants are born with a genetic potential for intelligence which is then either fostered or inhibited by life experiences."

c. "I'm examining the trait similarities between pairs of monozygotic twins."

d. "The results showed that 32 percent of the variation in neuroticism in my sample of participants is due to genetic factors."

Essay Questions

Write out answers to the following brief essay questions. Compare your responses with the sample answers at the end of the Study Guide chapter.

1. Explain why the author of your textbook considers the results of the Human Genome Project to represent a "landmark" achievement in the history of science.

2. What are the core principles of natural selection? List and describe each one.

3. One day while walking to class you overhear two professors discussing the topic of evolution and natural selection. One says, "Well, some human problems come from the fact that we are an ancient species living in a modern world." "Yes," the other professor agrees, "natural selection certainly is an imperfect process." Explain what the two professors are talking about, using examples from the text.

4. The results of one of the large-scale twin studies cited in your text indicate that heritability estimates of personality averaged around 48 percent. Define the concept of heritability and discuss how the twin study results can be used to support both the nature and the nurture perspectives on human development.

5. Describe the development of homosexuality according to Bem's "exotic becomes erotic" perspective.

TEST SOLUTIONS

Multiple-Choice Solutions

1. d (p. 297)	11. c (p. 306)	21. c (p. 315)
2. b (p. 297)	12. a (p. 306)	22. b (p. 315)
3. a (p. 299)	13. b (pp. 309-310)	23. d (p. 319)
4. c (p. 300)	14. a (pp. 309-310)	24. d (p. 320)
5. d (p. 302)	15. d (p. 309)	25. d (p. 321)
6. c (pp. 301-303)	16. c (p. 310)	26. c (p. 323)
7. a (p. 303)	17. d (p. 311)	27. b (p. 324)
8. b (p. 304)	18. d (p. 311)	28. d (p. 325)
9. d (p. 304)	19. a (p. 313)	29. a (p. 325)
10. c (p. 305)	20. c (p. 313)	30. a (p. 326)

True-False Solutions

1. T (p. 299)	6. T (p. 305)
2. T (p. 300)	7. F (p. 306)
3. F (p. 300)	8. T (p. 315)
4. F (p. 303)	9. F (p. 320)
5. T (p. 304)	10. T (p. 321)

Key Concepts Matching Solutions

Exercise #1	Exercise #2	Exercise #3
1. g	1. c	1. d
2. f	2. a	2. c
3. e	3. e	3. a
4. b	4. b	4. b
5. h	5. d	
6. a		
7. d		
8. c		

Essay Solutions

1. The results of the Human Genome Project represent a "landmark" achievement in the history of science for several reasons. First, the results provided evidence that people all around the world are extremely similar in terms of their basic genetic makeup. For example, 99.9 percent of the DNA letter sequences in the human genome are common to all humans (which means that only one tenth of one percent of the DNA letter sequences are responsible for the differences between us). This provides support for Darwin's evolutionary hypothesis that all humans originate from the same common ancestor. Second, scientists have been able to compare the human genome with the recently discovered mouse genome – with the result that we now know that humans and mice share 99 percent of the same genes. This also provides support for Darwin's hypothesis that humans share a common ancestor with other mammals. And third, additional research has revealed that despite the enormous genetic similarities among all humans, people tend to cluster into five genetic "groups" which correspond to the major geographical regions of the world. This finding suggests that there may be genetic differences among various racial and ethnic groups, which may help to explain the genetic underpinnings of region-specific diseases. (pp. 299-300)

2. There are several core principles of natural selection. First, within the species, individual organisms must vary; in other words, they cannot all be identical copies of each other. Second, some of the differences between individuals must confer survival benefits. That is, some of the individual organisms will be better suited in terms of their physical and psychological attributes to meet the demands of the environment. Third, the better-suited individuals must be more likely to survive and to reproduce. Fourth, the species must be capable of sexual reproduction (the transmittal of genetic material from parents to offspring). In this way, reproduction will perpetuate the genes and traits of better-suited organisms. (p. 302)

3. The professors are discussing two of the basic, and related, "facts" of natural selection. The second professor is pointing out that natural selection is not a conscious or premeditated process. Natural selection cannot look ahead and guess what the "perfect" human being will need to have by way of physical and psychological attributes for future life. Instead, natural selection must use the genetic material it has at hand – it is a reactive process. As a result, our adaptations are out of date; they lag behind changes in the environment. Thus, our minds and bodies are adapted for an ancestral environment – the highly social clan life of mobile, hunter-gatherer existence. There hasn't been enough time and no consistent environmental pressure for us to continue to evolve substantially since the time of our ancestors. The first professor is also making this point, but is more specifically implying that some of the experiences and problems that humans have today – like too much consumption of sweet and fatty foods (and corresponding high levels of obesity) and phobias to things that no longer pose significant threats to survival (spiders, snakes) – are the result of misfits or mismatches between human ancestral psychology and the contemporary environment. For example, in the ancestral environment, it was adaptive to eat as much food as possible since food was not readily available and humans who

125

displayed this behavior survived and reproduced (and "won" the evolutionary game). Contemporary humans have inherited this behavioral tendency or ancestral psychology, but it is no longer adaptive in an environment characterized by readily available food. (pp. 303, 306-308)

4. Heritability is a statistical estimate of the percentage of variation on a particular trait (or set of traits) that is due to genetic factors. The results of the twin studies clearly support the nature perspective. Approximately 48 percent of the variability in personality displayed by the twins in the study was accounted for by genetic factors. However, there is also clear evidence that environmental factors play a role in this aspect of human development. If personality were only caused by genetic factors, then the heritability estimate should be 100 percent. Thus, at least some of the variation in personality (up to 52 percent, in fact) is caused by environmental factors or by an interaction between genetic and environmental factors. (pp. 310-311, 313)

5. Bem believes that homosexuality arises from a psychobiological, developmental process. First, he argues that genes influence the temperament with which an individual is born; some infants (and children) will have a more active, energetic, aggressive temperament than others (i.e., a more stereotypically "masculine" temperament). These children will be drawn toward male playmates and so-called "masculine" activities; others will prefer female playmates and so-called "feminine" activities. Children who prefer same-sex playmates and gender-typical activities are "gender-conformists;" those who prefer opposite-sex playmates and gender atypical activities are "gender-nonconformists." The next stage of development is more psychological. Specifically, gender-conforming children come to see the opposite-sex as different, unfamiliar, and arousing ("exotic"); gender-nonconforming children come to view the same-sex that way ("exotic"). During puberty, as adolescents physically and sexually mature, they become attracted to whichever group of potential partners (same- or opposite-sex) is the most exotic; Bem calls this the "exotic becomes erotic" process. Although interesting, there is currently little evidence to support this theory. (pp. 326-327)

CHAPTER 9

HUMAN DEVELOPMENT

CHAPTER OVERVIEW

This chapter explores the biological, cognitive, and social aspects of development across the human life span. First, the goals of developmental psychology are discussed, along with the research strategies employed by developmental psychologists. The next section focuses on the unborn child, including the stages of prenatal development and the various factors (called teratogens) that can impede normal development. The chapter then considers the development of newborn babies – the research methods used to examine their abilities, their innate reflexes, their sensory capacities, and their sensitivity to number. Next, the chapter examines aspects of development during infancy and childhood. In turn, biological development (e.g., changes in the body), cognitive development (e.g., Piaget's theory, research on children's memory), and social development (e.g., parent-child attachment, peer relationships) are examined. The next section concerns adolescence. The various biological and physical events that mark this developmental stage are discussed, as are the cognitive changes (and corresponding alterations in moral reasoning) that occur. Aspects of social development are also examined, including changes in the parent-child relationship, the influence of peers, and sexuality. The chapter then turns to the topic of adulthood and old age, beginning with a consideration of the physical changes that mark adult development and the aging process. Cognitive development is examined (including age-related changes in memory and forgetting), and the impact of Alzheimer's disease on cognitive and physical function is addressed. The chapter then considers the topic of aging and intelligence, presenting research that indicates which forms of intelligence decline with age and which are unaffected by the aging process. Next, the critical events or turning points of adulthood, life satisfaction, and other aspects of social development are discussed. The chapter ends with a consideration of the psychological aspects of coping with dying and death.

CHAPTER OUTLINE

I. *What's Your Prediction* How Old Do People Feel?

II. Basic Developmental Questions

III. Prenatal Development

    A. The Growing Fetus

    B. *Psychology and Health* Does Alcohol Affect the Fetus?

IV. The Remarkable Newborn

    A. Reflexes

    B. Sensory Capacities
        1. Vision and visual preferences
        2. Hearing and auditory preferences

    C. *The Process of Discovery* Carolyn Rovee-Collier

    D. Sensitivity to Number

V. The Infant and Growing Child

    A. Biological Development
        1. Physical growth
        2. Motor skills

    B. Cognitive Development
        1. Piaget's theory
            a. Sensorimotor stage
            b. Preoperational stage
            c. Concrete operational stage
            d. Formal operational stage
            e. Piaget's legacy
        2. Information-processing perspectives

    C. Social Development
        1. The parent-child relationship
            a. The first attachment
            b. Styles of attachment
            c. The day-care controversy
        2. Peer relationships

VI. Adolescence

    A. Puberty

    B. Cognitive Development
        1. Moral reasoning

    C. Social and Personal Development
        1. Parent relationships
        2. Peer influences
        3. Sexuality

VII. Adulthood and Old Age

    A. Physical Changes in Adulthood
        1. The adult years
        2. Old age

    B. Aging and Intellectual Functions
        1. Memory and forgetting
        2. Alzheimer's disease
        3. Intelligence

    C. Social and Personal Development
        1. Ages and stages of adulthood
        2. Critical events of adulthood
        3. Changing perspectives on time

    D. Dying and Death

VIII. Thinking Like a Psychologist About Human Development

LEARNING OBJECTIVES

By the time you have read and reviewed this chapter, you should be able to:

1. Define developmental psychology and discuss the topics of interest to developmental psychologists (p. 333).

2. Compare cross-sectional and longitudinal research strategies (p. 333).

3. Outline the three stages of prenatal development (pp. 334-335). Define teratogens and discuss how specific factors (e.g., alcohol, drugs, AIDS virus) can impede normal prenatal development (pp. 335-337).

4. Define habituation and recovery and consider the various research techniques used to study very young infants (pp. 337-338).

5. Discuss the newborn infant's reflex capacities (p. 338). Consider the limitations and abilities that characterize the newborn infant's sensory systems (pp. 338-341).

6. Consider whether infants are born with an innate sensitivity to numbers (p. 341).

7. Explain the biological changes that occur during infancy and early childhood (pp. 342-343). Explain how the body and brain change during this period of development (pp. 343-343). Consider the changes in motor skill that occur (p. 343).

8. Explain Piaget's theory of cognitive development (pp. 343-348). Define the process of assimilation and accommodation (pp. 343-344). Consider the major cognitive limitations and milestones that characterize the sensorimotor, preoperational, concrete operational, and formal operational stages of development (pp. 344-348).

9. Examine the contributions made by, and the criticisms of, Piagetian cognitive theory (pp. 347-348). Compare Piaget's theory with the information-processing theory of cognitive development (pp. 348-349). Discuss the changes in memory that occur during early childhood (p. 349).

10. Discuss social development in infancy and early childhood (pp. 349-354). Explain the difference between imprinting and attachment (p. 350).

11. Consider the significance of the Harlow monkey studies for the study of attachment (pp. 350-351).

12. Explain the strange-situation test (p. 351). Consider the difference between a secure and an insecure attachment style (p. 351). Discuss the importance of the first attachment (p. 352).

13. Discuss the controversy over day-care versus home-care of children (pp. 352-353).

14. Explain the concept of horizontal relationships (p. 353). Discuss the peer relationship patterns of infants and young children (p. 353). Consider the importance of friendship formation (p. 353).

15. Define adolescence (p. 354). Consider the biological milestones associated with the transition to adolescence (pp. 355-356). Compare boys' and girls' development during puberty (pp. 355-356). Discuss factors that influence boys' and girls' reactions to puberty (p. 356).

16. Consider the cognitive changes that occur during adolescence (p. 356). Consider how cognitive changes influence changes in moral reasoning (pp. 356-358).

17. Outline Kohlberg's theory of moral development (p. 357). Discuss three major criticisms of Kohlberg's theory and consider alternative theories of morality (pp. 357-358).

18. Consider the social crises (e.g., identity crisis) that characterize adolescence (pp. 358-359). Outline how the parent-child relationship changes during adolescence (pp. 359-360).

19. Discuss peer influences during adolescence (p. 360).

20. Examine the changes in sexuality that mark adolescence (pp. 360-361). Explain why many teenagers do not use contraception (p. 361).

21. Distinguish between the human life span and the average human life expectancy (p. 362). Describe the physical changes that mark adult development and aging (pp. 362-364).

22. Discuss changes in memory and forgetting that occur as we age (pp. 364-365). Discuss two neurocognitive reasons for age-related declines in memory (pp. 364-365).

23. Define Alzheimer's disease (AD) and describe the cognitive effects of this progressive brain disorder (p. 365).

24. Examine the relation between aging and changes in various types of intelligence (pp. 365-366).

25. Describe Levinson's four eras of adulthood (pp. 367-368).

26. Examine the critical events of adulthood (pp. 368-369). Define the concept of social clock and explain its purpose (p. 368).

27. Consider the ways in which both the perception and the management of time change as people age (p. 369).

28. List and describe the five stages of coping with death and dying (p. 369). Consider whether all people pass through the five stages in the same sequence (pp. 369-370).

KEY TERMS

The following key terms and concepts are featured in this chapter and are important for you to know. Write out definitions of each term and check your answers with the definitions in the text on the pages listed.

Developmental psychology (p. 333)
Cross-sectional study (p. 333)
Longitudinal study (p. 333)
Zygote (p. 334)
Embryo (p. 335)
Fetus (p. 335)
Teratogens (p. 335)
Fetal alcohol syndrome (FAS) (p. 337)
Habituation (p. 337)
Recovery (p. 337)
Grasping reflex (p. 338)
Rooting reflex (p. 338)
Schemas (p. 343)
Assimilation (p. 343)
Accommodation (p. 343)

TEST QUESTIONS

Multiple-Choice Questions

Circle the correct choice for each question and compare your answers with those at the end of the Study Guide chapter.

1. A central concern for developmental psychology is
    a. how people grow and change across the life span.
    b. the genetic basis of personality.
    c. how human behavior is affected by the social environment.
    d. the treatment of abnormal behavior.

2. In order to examine whether age is related to reasoning ability, Dr. Mathers gives the Reasoning Ability Test to a group of individuals ranging in age from 20 to 50 years old. He finds that the younger age groups outperform the older age groups. What kind of study is this?
   a. experimental
   b. cross-sectional
   c. descriptive case study
   d. longitudinal

3. What should Dr. Mathers be concerned about when he interprets his results?
   a. cohort effects
   b. the logistics of conducting this kind of study
   c. the lack of correlation
   d. All of the above

4. The first stage in prenatal development is called the _____ stage.
   a. embryonic
   b. zygotic
   c. germinal
   d. fetal

5. All major body structures form during the _____ stage of prenatal development.
   a. germinal
   b. embryonic
   c. fetal
   d. zygotic

6. Which substance can function as a teratogen?
   a. aspirin
   b. cocaine
   c. x-rays
   d. All of the above

7. At a pediatric clinic, you notice a young child who seems very small for her age. Her nose is flattened, her eyes are wide apart, and she seems to be slightly mentally retarded. This child may have
   a. cocaine abuse syndrome.
   b. fetal alcohol syndrome.
   c. x-ray exposure.
   d. nicotine syndrome.

8. Why is the measurement of habituation and recovery important in conducting research on infants?
   a. It allows infants to vocally indicate their preferences for things.
   b. It allows researchers to communicate with very young infants.
   c. It allows infants to develop their sucking reflex skills.
   d. It allow researchers to determine when infants can make distinctions between different stimuli.

9. Which one of the following reflexes is innate?
   a. rooting
   b. sucking
   c. grasping
   d. All of the above

10. Little Nancy is fascinated by the kitten playing on the floor nearby and does not take her eyes off him. When the kitten passes behind Nancy, however, she makes no attempt to turn around toward him. Nancy
    a. has a visual problem.
    b. lacks object permanence.
    c. is not yet in the sensorimotor stage.
    d. is mentally retarded.

11. The little girl who insists that her sister does not have a sister is demonstrating
    a. separation anxiety.
    b. egocentric thinking.
    c. conservation.
    d. formal operational thinking.

12. Three-year-old Miko is very upset. His dad gave him and his friend each a cookie. However, his friend's cookie broke in half. Miko is convinced that his friend now has more cookie than he himself has. Miko's misunderstanding is due to
    a. the absence of object permanence.
    b. egocentric thinking.
    c. lack of conservation.
    d. abstract logic.

13. In general, research indicates that Piaget was incorrect in his estimates of the _____ of development, but correct in his estimates of the _____ of development.
    a. overall rate; sequential achievements
    b. sequential achievements; overall rate
    c. age periods; overall rate
    d. measurement; thought processes

14. According to the information processing perspective, the difference in the problem-solving abilities of a two-year-old and a five-year-old is due primarily to
    a. differences in social skills.
    b. differences in selective attention and memory.
    c. the differences in their language abilities.
    d. the increase in the ability to conserve and to reason abstractly.

15. The very deep emotional bond that forms between infants and their caregivers is called
    a. attachment.
    b. imprinting.
    c. critical bonding.
    d. a horizontal relationship.

16. An infant cries when her father leaves the room, and also when a stranger is in the room. When the father returns, the baby is all smiles and hugs. This infant is
    a. imprinted on her father.
    b. insecurely attached to strangers.
    c. securely attached to her father.
    d. insecurely attached to her mother.

17. The key factor that seems to determine how day care affects young children is the _____.
    a. amount of time a child spends in day care
    b. quality of the time spent in day care
    c. type of parent-child attachment
    d. number of siblings in the home

18. Adolescence begins with a(n) _____ event.
    a. biological
    b. emotional
    c. cognitive
    d. social

19. In girls, early puberty often is associated with _____; in boys, early puberty tends to be related to _____.
    a. personal benefits; interpersonal benefits
    b. adjustment difficulties; social benefits
    c. interpersonal benefits; adjustment difficulties
    d. positive adjustment; negative adjustment

20. Michelle believes that we should help others because "by helping others, you avoid dishonor and people will respect you and look up to you." Michelle is at the _____ level of moral reasoning.
    a. preconventional
    b. conventional
    c. postconventional
    d. social conventional

21. Nick is willing to let other students copy his old papers – but only if he is offered enough money. This exemplifies _____ moral reasoning.
    a. preconventional
    b. conventional
    c. postconventional
    d. unconventional

22. At what age are most people operating at a postconventional level of moral reasoning?
    a. 7
    b. 13
    c. 16
    d. none of the above

23. According to Erikson, the transitional period of adolescence is marked by a(n) _____ crisis.
    a. sexual
    b. cognitive
    c. identity
    d. moral

24. Which person is most likely to conform to the influence of friends?
    a. Tommy, a second-grader
    b. Tammy, a sixth-grader
    c. Timmy, a ninth-grader
    d. Tuppence, a college student

25. Research suggests that adolescent risk-taking is a function of:
    a. rebelliousness.
    b. reacting to social situations that call for risk.
    c. increased opportunities to engage in "adult" behaviors.
    d. All of the above

26. Among humans, life expectancy is influenced by
    a. genetics.
    b. nutrition.
    c. personality factors.
    d. All of the above

27. Research suggests that _____ declines and _____ remains relatively stable across the life span.
    a. crystallized intelligence; fluid intelligence.
    b. fluid intelligence; crystallized intelligence
    c. reasoning ability; mental speed
    d. mental speed; wisdom

28. According to Erikson's model of social development, for young adults it is critical to find _____.
    a. identity
    b. generativity
    c. intimacy
    d. integrity

29. "It's time for you to settle down," Bill's mother is fond of telling him. "All of my friends' children are married and raising children of their own. Why don't you go out and meet someone nice…" These statements reflect the existence of
    a. a social clock.
    b. parent-child conflict.
    c. a social crisis.
    d. intimacy vs. isolation.

30. Which of the following stages are individuals likely to pass through as they cope with the knowledge of death?
    a. depression
    b. anger
    c. denial
    d. All of the above

True-False Questions

Indicate which of the following statements are true or false, and compare your answers with those at the end of the chapter.

T F 1. In the womb, the unborn child is protected from all environmental influences.

T F 2. Research suggests that human infants are born with a special orientation toward the face.

T F 3. The process of myelination in the brain stops after the second year of life.

T F 4. Piaget's first three stages of cognitive development occur in children from different cultures at roughly the same time.

T F 5. There is a critical period for the development of attachment.

T F 6. Almost all horizontal relationships in childhood are between members of the same sex.

T F 7. Many cultures have initiation rites to celebrate the passage from childhood to adulthood.

T F 8. Kohlberg's model of moral development may be most applicable to urban societies.

T F 9. All types of intelligence decrease with age.

T F 10. In the 1950's most Americans believed that men and women should marry at the ages of 19 and 24.

Key Concepts Matching Exercises

Exercise #1: Cognitive Development

Place the developmental milestones and concepts on the right into the correct Piagetian stage listed on the left. Note that more than one concept will "fit" into each stage!

_____ 1. Sensorimotor

_____ 2. Preoperational

_____ 3. Concrete operations

_____ 4. Formal operations

a. "A cup of water is still a cup of water, no matter what size container you put it in."

b. this stage usually occurs during adolescence and adulthood

c. this stage is marked by intuitive, prelogical thinking

d. "Out of sight, out of mind."

e. "If I close my eyes, you won't be able to see me."

f. separation anxiety

g. this stage usually spans years two to six

h. knowledge of the world is gained by touching, tasting, smelling, and manipulating objects

i. verbal skills develop rapidly during this stage

j. systematic hypothesis testing becomes possible during this stage.

k. this stage is marked by a lack of conservation

l. research reveals cross-cultural differences in the development of this stage

m. this stage is marked by the development of logical reasoning

n. "What you see is what you get."

o. egocentrism is a hallmark of this stage

p. spans about ages six to twelve

Exercise #2: Kohlberg's Theory of Moral Development

Place the motivations and statements on the right into the correct stage of moral development listed on the left.

_____ 1. Preconventional morality

_____ 2. Conventional morality

_____ 3. Postconventional morality

a. revolves around the motivation to fulfill one's duty to society and to avoid feelings of guilt
b. "Stealing is bad. When you steal, you get in trouble."
c. "Stealing is bad. When you steal, you break the law, and we all should follow the law."
d. revolves around the motivation to avoid punishment
e. "I had to steal. I know it was against the law, but sometimes laws must be broken. By stealing, I was able to do what my conscience tells me is right."
f. revolves around the motivation to gain approval and avoid disapproval
g. "I would never steal. After all, I have a reputation to uphold. What would other people think if I were to be caught stealing?"
h. involves the motivation to uphold one's own ethical principles and values
i. involves the motivation to obtain rewards

j. "I help people because it's my duty to do so. I would feel so guilty if I saw someone in need and didn't stop to offer assistance."
k. "I help my brother because my parents praise me when I do."
l. involves the motivation to maintain and follow social principles

Exercise #3: Coping With Death and Dying

Match the statements on the right with the five stages in the coping process listed on the left.

_____ 1. Denial

_____ 2. Anger

_____ 3. Bargaining

_____ 4. Depression

_____ 5. Acceptance

a. "If I pull through this, I will exercise every day and I will never yell at my family again."

b. "Well, there's not much I can do about this now. I guess what has to be, will be."

c. "This is so unfair! Why do these things always happen to me? I could just scream!"

d. "It's all over. My life is meaningless. I just want to be left alone."

e. "This is not happening to me. The doctors must be wrong."

Essay Questions

Write out answers to the following brief essay questions. Compare your responses with the sample answers at the end of the Study Guide chapter.

1. What are the two basic approaches for studying developmental processes? Compare and contrast these two approaches. What are the problems associated with each one?

2. Are infants "minimathematicians"? Discuss the research by Winn on sensitivity to number in infants.

3. Horizontal relationships with peers become an important aspect of social development in childhood. Discuss the four types of children who have been identified based on the sociometric method. Why are these friendship patterns and peer evaluations important?

4. When four-year-old Lyle sees his little sister fall down and start to cry, he runs over to her and offers her his "blankie." His aunts disagree over the meaning of Lyle's behavior. Auntie Eleanor says, "Oh look, Lyle feels sorry for Becky. He wants to make her feel better and so he's giving her his blanket." Auntie Mildred disagrees. "Children are incapable of that sort of higher moral thinking. Lyle knows that we'll reward him if he behaves nicely to his sister." According to Kohlberg's theory of moral reasoning who is more likely to be right?

5. A common stereotype of the elderly is that they are absentminded. What changes occur in memory and forgetting as we age? What are two neurocognitive bases for these age-related changes?

TEST SOLUTIONS

Multiple-Choice Solutions

1. a (p. 333)	11. b (pp. 345-346)	21. a (p. 357)
2. b (p. 333)	12. c (p. 346)	22. d (p. 357)
3. a (p. 333)	13. a (pp. 347-348)	23. c (pp. 358-359)
4. c (p. 334)	14. b (p. 348)	24. c (p. 360)
5. b (p. 335)	15. a (p. 350)	25. d (p. 361)
6. d (p. 335)	16. c (p. 351)	26. d (p. 362)
7. b (p. 336)	17. b (p. 353)	27. b (p. 366)
8. d (p. 337)	18. a (p. 354)	28. c (p. 367)
9. d (p. 338)	19. b (p. 356)	29. a (p. 368)
10. b (p. 345)	20. b (p. 357)	30. d (p. 369)

True-False Solutions

1. F (p. 335)	6. T (p. 353)
2. T (p. 340)	7. T (p. 354)
3. F (p. 342)	8. T (p. 357)
4. T (p. 347)	9. F (p. 366)
5. F (p. 350)	10. T (p. 368)

Key Concepts Matching Solutions

Exercise #1	Exercise #2	Exercise #3
1. d, f, h	1. b, d, i, k	1. e
2. c, e, g, i, k, n, o	2. a, f, g, j	2. c
3. a, m, p	3. c, e, h, l	3. a
4. b, j, l		4. d
		5. b

Essay Solutions

1. Cross-sectional studies involve examining people of different ages at the same point in time and then comparing their responses. For example, a researcher might measure the IQ of a number of people of varying ages and then see whether IQ and age are correlated. The major problem with this type of study (aside from the fact that it is correlational and therefore cannot be used to demonstrate causality) is that of cohort effects. A cohort effect occurs when there are preexisting differences between generations or age groups (called cohorts). A researcher who finds that older adults reason differently from younger adults might conclude that there are age differences in reasoning ability; but these differences might be due to the fact that one cohort spent less time in school than the other cohort. (p. 333)

   The second method is the longitudinal study, which involves following the same group of participants over time and testing them repeatedly. For example, a researcher might measure reasoning ability in the same group of people during their 10th year, 15th year, and 20th year of life. This strategy allows the researcher to measure change over time, something the cross-sectional study cannot do. However, on the downside, this strategy takes a great deal of time and requires long-term cooperation from participants. (p. 333)

2. There is some research evidence that infants may be born with an innate sensitivity to numbers. Wynn found that five-month-olds had a rudimentary ability to add and subtract. She demonstrated this by showing them one or two Mickey Mouse dolls being put on a stage and then covered by a screen. Next, they saw her add a doll to the one behind the screen, or take one away. Babies looked longer at the incorrect outcomes, apparently because these outcomes were unexpected (p. 341).

3. Teachers have identified four types of school-age children based on their "sociometric" status among peers (this method involves asking the children to rate themselves and to nominate the classmates they like the most and the least). Children can be classified as popular (sociable, skilled, and well liked), rejected (aggressive or withdrawn, lacking social skills, and disliked), controversial (sociable, often aggressive, liked and disliked), and neglected (less sociable and aggressive than average, seldom mentioned by peers). These peer ratings appear to have important correlates. For example, popular children have the most friends and thus have access to the benefit of these friendships. Rejected children seem to be the most at risk--they are more likely to be lonely, to drop out of school, and to have academic difficulties and social adjustment problems as adults. Thus, friendships seem to provide a child with certain developmental advantages. (pp. 353-354)

4. According to Kohlberg's theory Auntie Mildred is more likely to be right. Auntie Mildred is espousing the traditional Kohlberg view that young children resolve moral dilemmas in ways that reflect self-serving motives. Mildred views Lyle's act of kindness as motivated out of his desire to obtain rewards. Children as young as Lyle would almost certainly be functioning at the preconventional level of moral development (p. 357).

5. There are several age-related changes in cognitive function that occur. For example, older adults are less able than younger adults to free-recall previously learned information (although their recognition memory appears unimpaired) (p. 364).

Two neurocognitive phenomena may explain these changes. The first has to do with sensory acuity. Specifically, as people age, their eyesight and hearing become increasingly impaired; this may influence their ability to perform a variety of cognitive tasks. The second neurocognitive factor that is implicated in these memory changes concerns neural speed. As people age, they process and react to information more slowly; this neural speed loss impairs performance on a range of cognitive tasks (since it takes more time to process information, people have less time to actually rehearse that information) (pp. 364-365).

CHAPTER 10

MOTIVATION AND EMOTION

CHAPTER OVERVIEW

The topic of this chapter is motivation and emotion. Your textbook author first defines the concept of motivation, and then explores the various theories that have been advanced to explain and account for motivated behavior. In turn, the chapter compares and contrasts general theories of motivation (i.e., instinct theories, drive theory, arousal theory, and incentive theory), as well as Maslow's hierarchy of needs explanation for motivation. Then, specific human motives are examined, beginning with basic motives (i.e., hunger, sex). First, the biological and psychological aspects of hunger and eating are discussed, as well as some consequences of the hunger motive (e.g., obesity, eating disorders). Then, a second basic motivation, sexual motivation, is explored. The next section of the chapter focuses on social motives. First, two distinct motives having to do with the need to belong are examined. Specifically, the personal and situational factors that influence the need for affiliation and the need for intimacy are discussed. Esteem motives such as the need for achievement, also are examined. In the second half of the chapter the concept of emotion is defined, and then the chapter examines each of the three components that interact to produce emotional experiences. Specifically, the physiological or bodily sensations that are involved in emotion are examined, including the various brain centers (i.e., limbic system, cerebral cortex) and nervous systems (i.e., sympathetic, parasympathetic) that play an important role in emotion regulation. Next, the chapter turns to the expressive component of emotional experiences, beginning with an examination of the way in which our outward expressions of emotion can nonverbally communicate to others and to ourselves about how we feel. The question of whether some emotions and emotional expressions are "basic" or innate is examined, along with research that suggests that our own facial expressions can actually trigger an emotional experience (e.g., we smile, and then we feel happy). The cognitive component of emotion then is explored. The chapter presents Schachter's two-factor theory of emotion, and the cognitive appraisals associated with various emotions are explored, as is the impact of counterfactual thinking (the tendency to imagine alternative outcomes that might have occurred but did not) on emotional experience. This section ends with a discussion of whether cognition is a necessary component of emotion and whether people can predict their future emotional states. The chapter then segues into a consideration of different types of emotions and how a few basic human emotions can combine to produce the vast array of feelings we experience. The chapter ends with a consideration of happiness and the conditions that produce a state of subjective well-being.

CHAPTER OUTLINE

I. *What's Your Prediction* Can Culture Influence Emotion?

II. What Motivates Us?

    A. General Theories of Motivation
        1. Drive theory
        2. Arousal theory
        3. Incentive theory

    B. The Pyramid of Human Motivations

III. Basic Human Motives

    A. Hunger and Eating
        1. The biological component
        2. Psychological influences
        3. Obesity
            a. What causes obesity?
            b. How to lose weight
        4. Eating disorders

    B. Sexual Motivation
        1. Surveys of sexual practices
        2. The evolution of desire

    C. *The Process of Discovery* David M. Buss

IV. Social Motives

    A. Belongingness Motives
        1. The need for affiliation
        2. The need for intimacy

    B. Esteem Motives
        1. The need for achievement

V. Emotion

VI. The Physiological Component

    A. A Historical Perspective

    B. Brain Centers of Emotion

LEARNING OBJECTIVES

By the time you have read and reviewed this chapter, you should be able to:

1. Define the concept of motivation and contrast the two major ways in which psychologists have approached this subject (pp. 376-377).

2. Compare the four general theories of human motivation (i.e., instinct, drive, arousal, and incentive). Explain the basic tenets of each of these theories (pp. 377-379).

3. Discuss Maslow's hierarchy of needs theory of human motivation. Explain the importance of the pyramid structure in terms of understanding human needs. Compare this approach with the general theories of motivation (p. 379).

4. Examine the biological components of the basic motive of hunger. Discuss the role played by the stomach, brain, and autonomic nervous system in regulating hunger (pp. 380-381).

5. Consider the importance of psychological factors in regulating hunger, including taste, smell, visual cues, cultural experience, and social cues (the presence of others) (pp. 381-382).

6. Discuss the consequences of the hunger motive, including obesity and eating disorders (pp. 382-386). Consider the causes of obesity and how it may be treated (pp. 383-385). Examine the causes of eating disorders (pp. 385-386).

7. Explain the consequences of the sexual motive for the species and the individual (p. 386).

8. Summarize survey research on sexual practices, and discuss sex differences in sexual behavior (pp. 386-387).

9. Consider the evolutionary explanation for sex differences in sexual behavior (pp. 387-388). Explain the psychological explanation for the same differences (p. 388).

10. Define belongingness needs and the two types of belongingness motives (i.e., affiliation and intimacy) (pp. 390-391).

11. Explain the need for affiliation (p. 390). Consider individual differences in this motive as well as social factors that influence the need to affiliate (e.g., stress) (pp. 390-391).

12. Define the need for intimacy (p. 391). Explain how self-disclosure is related to the need for intimacy (p. 391). Consider sex differences in self-disclosure and the relationship between self-disclosure and relationship satisfaction (p. 391).

13. Explain the need for achievement and consider ways to measure this motive (pp. 392-393). Explore the association among the need for achievement, actual behavior, and level of accomplishment (p. 392). Explain how the attributions that people make for their successes and failures impact their subsequent achievement efforts (pp. 392-393).

14 Define the concept of emotion and identify the three components of emotional experience (p. 394).

15. Discuss the physiological component of emotion (pp. 394-398).

16. Compare and contrast the James-Lange and Cannon-Bard theories of emotion (p. 395).

17. Discuss the role played by the brain (i.e., limbic system, cerebral cortex) and nervous system (i.e., parasympathetic, sympathetic systems) in the regulation of emotion (pp. 395-396).

18. Consider whether each emotion has its own specific pattern of physiological arousal or whether all emotions are accompanied by the same general state of arousal (pp. 396-398).

19. Consider the expressive component of emotion (p. 398). Discuss the two functions served by the behavioral expression of emotion (p. 398).

20. Explain how emotional states are communicated by facial expression and consider the adaptive significance of the ability to recognize emotion via facial expression (pp. 398-400).

21. Define the facial-feedback hypothesis (pp. 401-402). Explain how facial expression and body posture actually may trigger or cause an emotional experience (p. 402).

22. Consider the cognitive component of emotion (pp. 402-403). Define Schachter's two-factor theory of emotion (pp. 403-404).

23. Define the concept of counterfactual thinking (p. 404). Discuss how counterfactual thinking may influence the experience of emotion (pp. 404-405).

24. Consider the debate over whether cognition is a necessary component of emotion (pp. 405-407).

25. Discuss the concept of affective forecasting and consider whether people can accurately predict their future emotional states (p. 407). Define the durability bias and explain two reasons for this bias in affective forecasting (p. 407).

26. Explain how emotions can be classified and compared along the dimensions of pleasantness and intensity (pp. 408-409).

27. Discuss cultural differences in the types of antecedent events that cause various emotions, the words used to describe emotional experiences, and the display rules that govern the expression of emotion (pp. 409-410).

28. Discuss the factors that are correlated with feelings of happiness (p. 410). Summarize survey research on the prevalence of happiness (p. 410). Consider the relationship between income and subjective well-being (pp. 411-412).

KEY TERMS

The following key terms and concepts are featured in this chapter and are important for you to know. Write out definitions of each term and check your answers with the definitions in the text on the pages listed.

Motivation (p. 376)
Instinct (p. 377)
Drive theory (p. 377)
Arousal theory (p. 378)
Incentive theory (p. 378)
Hierarchy of needs (p. 379)
Obesity (p. 382)
Set point (p. 384)
Anorexia nervosa (p. 385)
Bulimia nervosa (p. 386)
Need for affiliation (p. 390)
Need for intimacy (p. 390)
Self-disclosure (p. 391)
Achievement motivation (p. 392)
Emotion (p. 394)
James-Lange theory (p. 395)
Cannon-Bard theory (p. 395)
Sympathetic nervous system (p. 396)
Parasympathetic nervous system (p. 396)
Facial electromyograph (EMG) (p. 400)
Facial-feedback hypothesis (p. 402)
Two-factor theory of emotion (p. 403)
Counterfactual thinking (p. 404
Affective forecasting (p. 407)

TEST QUESTIONS

Multiple-Choice Questions

Circle the correct choice for each question and compare your answers with those at the end of the Study Guide chapter.

1. Which of the following are considered to be human needs or motives?
   a. hunger
   b. affiliation
   c. power
   d. All of the above

2. Dr. Dewey is an avid believer in the instinct theory of motivation. He is specifically interested in the aggression instinct. What is the title of his book most likely to be?
   a. "Aggression: The Drive to Reduce Tension"
   b. "Aggression: Hard-Wired by Evolution"
   c. "Aggression: How to Optimize Your Level"
   d. "Aggression: Expected Outcomes and You"

3. Rebecca prefers calm situations and risk-free activities, Jesse enjoys somewhat stimulating situations and moderately risky activities, and Nick craves intense experiences and high-risk activities. The differences between these three individuals are best explained by the _____ theory of motivation.
   a. instinct
   b. drive
   c. arousal
   d. incentive

4. Drive theory suggests that humans are _____ into action by internal needs, whereas incentive theory suggests that humans are _____ into action by external goals.
   a. forced; pushed
   b. pushed; pulled
   c. pulled; pushed
   d. pushed; prodded

5. Tilly has met all of her basic, physiological needs. According to Maslow's hierarchy of needs, what need or needs will Tilly strive to fulfill next?
   a. needs for food and water
   b. needs for safety and financial security
   c. needs for affiliation and affection
   d. need for esteem

6. Which of the following biological structures or processes does not appear to have an important role in the regulation of hunger?
   a. the lateral hypothalamus
   b. the ventromedial hypothalamus
   c. the liver
   d. stomach contractions

7. The _____ hypothalamus seems to be the brain's "hunger center"; when it is stimulated, an animal will eat even when he or she is full.
   a. ventrical
   b. lateral
   c. ventromedial
   d. basal

8. Casey recently was involved in an accident in which part of his brain was destroyed. Before his accident, he was of average weight and had no trouble regulating his appetite. Now, he complains of feeling hungry all the time, and he eats larger and larger quantities of food. He has already doubled his body weight. Most likely, the brain area that was destroyed was the
   a. brainstem.
   b. lateral hypothalamus.
   c. ventromedial hypothalamus.
   d. cortex.

9. Which of the following are considered external food cues?
   a. the time of day
   b. the smell of food
   c. the taste of food
   d. All of the above

10. Which one of the following statements about obesity is accurate?
    a. Being even slightly overweight poses an extremely serious health risk.
    b. Obesity is linked with diabetes, heart disease, sleep apnea, and depression.
    c. Few stereotypes about obese individuals exist.
    d. Body size preferences do not differ across cultures.

11. Both Lotty and Lonny are on the gymnastics team at school. Lotty is very concerned about her weight and spends over two hours each day exercising. She also follows a very restrictive diet and appears thin and emaciated. Lonny is equally concerned about his weight and also spends a good deal of time exercising. However, he maintains his weight by eating as much as he wants and then using laxatives and self-induced vomiting to purge the food from his body. Lotty may have a condition called _____, whereas Lonny probably has _____.
    a. compulsive dieting; compulsive overeating
    b. purge syndrome; binge syndrome
    c. anorexia nervosa; bulimia nervosa
    d. exercise-induced starvation; obesity phobia

12. Dawn refers to herself as a "people person." She sends letters, places calls, and arranges frequent parties in order to maintain contact with her many friends. Dawn probably has a
    a. social disorder.
    b. high need for affiliation.
    c. low need for intimacy.
    d. belongingness need.

13. Flynn prefers to spend time with one close friend as opposed to a group of acquaintances. He particularly enjoys the deep affection and self-disclosure that characterize his close friendships. Flynn probably has a high need for
    a. intimacy.
    b. reciprocity.
    c. friendship.
    d. affiliation.

14. Research on sex differences in self-disclosure reveals that
    a. men disclose more to others than do women.
    b. women receive less self-disclosure from others than do men.
    c. men disclose less to others than do women.
    d. women and men are equally open in their communication styles.

15. Ever since he was a child, Pietro has been competitive – both with himself and with others. In college, he double-majored and took the most difficult classes in each area. At the office, he handles his firm's most difficult cases, and he works longer hours than any other partner. On the street where he lives, his yard is the neatest and his garden yields the most produce. These behaviors demonstrate a high level of
    a. success.
    b. esteem.
    c. achievement motivation.
    d. need for power.

16. In general, psychologists agree that all emotions consist of which of the following components?
    a. internal physiological arousal
    b. expressive behavior
    c. cognitive appraisal
    d. All of the above

17. According to the James-Lange theory of emotions,
    a. emotion triggers a physiological response.
    b. physiological and behavioral responses trigger emotion.
    c. emotion triggers a behavioral reaction.
    d. physiological responses trigger emotions, which in turn trigger behavioral responses.

18. Cannon and Bard criticized the James-Lange theory on the grounds that
    a. bodily sensations alone do not always produce emotion.
    b. specific emotions are not associated with specific physical changes.
    c. emotion is sometimes felt instantly, before the body has undergone any physical change.
    d. All of the above

19. The _____ regulates several emotions, including fear.
    a. limbic system
    b. brainstem
    c. sympathetic nervous system
    d. spinal cord

20. During an emotional event, the _____ prepares the body for action. After an emotional event, the _____ returns the body to its pre-mobilized state.
    a. cerebral cortex; limbic system
    b. left hemisphere; right hemisphere
    c. sympathetic system; parasympathetic system
    d. autonomic nervous system; cerebral cortex

21. According to the Darwinian or evolutionary perspective on emotions, people should be especially sensitive to signs of _____ from another person.
    a. happiness
    b. anger
    c. neutrality
    d. joy

22. Vincent and Don are listening to a political candidate speak about a highly controversial issue. Vincent is strongly interested in what the speaker has to say and pleasantly surprised by her knowledge of the opposing viewpoint. Don is bothered by the issue being discussed and angered at the candidate's portrayal of the opposing viewpoint. A facial EMG of Vincent would reveal increased activity in the _____; a facial EMG of Don would indicate increased activity in the _____.
    a. cheek muscles; forehead and brow area
    b. mouth area; cheek and eye area
    c. left half of the face; right half of the face
    d. right hemisphere; left hemisphere

23. According to the facial-feedback hypothesis, facial expressions activate emotion through a process of _____.
    a. self-perception
    b. social comparison
    c. cognitive appraisal
    d. misattribution

24. The two-factor theory of emotion states that we will feel a particular emotion
    a. whenever we become physiologically aroused.
    b. whenever those around us act in an emotional manner.
    c. when we are physiologically aroused and the situation provides us with an appropriate emotional label for our arousal.
    d. when we take drugs.

25. Brett was recently involved in a car accident. "Gee," he thinks, "the repairs are going to be expensive, but it could have been so much worse. At least nobody was injured." Brett is engaging in _____.
    a. counterfactual thinking
    b. self-perception
    c. social comparison
    d. cognitive appraisal

26. Emotions that are considered "basic" are those that
    a. are accompanied by a distinct facial expression.
    b. are displayed by infants and young children.
    c. are experienced by people from diverse cultures.
    d. All of the above

27. Which of the following are considered to be "basic" emotions?
    a. surprise
    b. fear
    c. joy
    d. All of the above

28. Research reveals striking cultural differences in the _____ of emotion.
    a. physiological components
    b. display rules
    c. expressive components
    d. facial expression

29. Survey data reveal that roughly _____ percent of the American population describe themselves as happy.
    a. 25
    b. 50
    c. 75
    d. 95

30. Research on happiness reveals that subjective well-being is not related to
    a. age.
    b. health.
    c. employment status.
    d. social relationships.

True-False Questions

Indicate which of the following statements are true or false, and compare your answers with those at the end of the chapter.

T F   1. Modern psychologists have rejected instinct theories of motivation.

T F   2. Drive theory is best able to explain biologically (as opposed to socially) driven behavior.

T F   3. Research indicates that all people ascend Maslow's hierarchy of needs in the same order.

T F   4. Eating and hunger are subject to both biological and social influences.

T F   5. Stress can increase the need to affiliate.

T F   6. Emotions in general consist of a physiological, expressive, and cognitive component.

T F   7. During an emotional event, the hypothalamus activates that sympathetic nervous system.

T F   8. Positive emotions are associated with characteristic activity in the cheek muscles.

T F   9. Cognition appears to have little influence on emotional experience.

T F   10. Some emotions are more "basic" than others.

Key Concepts Matching Exercises

Exercise #1: Motivation

Match the key terms on the left with the definitions on the right.

_____ 1. Drive theory
_____ 2. Arousal theory
_____ 3. Incentive theory
_____ 4. Set point
_____ 5. Anorexia nervosa
_____ 6. Bulimia nervosa
_____ 7. Need for affiliation
_____ 8. Need for intimacy
_____ 9. Self-disclosure
_____ 10. Achievement motivation

a. the need for close, intimate relationships characterized by open communication

b. "I must succeed. Give me the hardest tasks, and then watch me outperform all the others."

c. an eating disorder in which a person limits food intake and becomes thinner than normal

d. this is the need to establish and maintain social contacts

e. "I'm hungry. I'm irritable. I don't like feeling this way. I'm going to get some food."

f. an eating disorder that is characterized by episodes of binge eating and purging

g. "I'll share my thoughts with you, and then you can share yours with me."

h. the notion that people are motivated to obtain a valued outcome

i. "No matter what I do, I seem to stay at the same weight."

j. "There were just too many people at that party. It was fun, but now I need some down time."

Exercise #2: Emotion

Match the key terms on the left with the definitions on the right.

_____ 1. James-Lange theory
_____ 2. Cannon-Bard theory
_____ 3. Facial-feedback hypothesis
_____ 4. Two-factor theory
_____ 5. Misattribution

a. "I'm so happy that I made that decision. The alternative could have been so much worse."

b. "That huge spider just came right at me! I ran away as fast as I could. I can still feel my heart pounding – I'm terrified!"

c. I'm feeling kind of tense and aroused. That guy over there looks scared. I must be feeling "scared, too."

d. "When the big, hairy spider jumped out at me, my pulse began to race, my knees went weak, and I was overcome with terror – all at the same terrible moment."

e. "I'm smiling, so I must be having a good time."

Essay Questions

Write out answers to the following brief essay questions. Compare your responses with the sample answers at the end of the Study Guide chapter.

1. Chance likes to live up to his name by taking chances and engaging in daredevil activities like skydiving, parasailing, and bungee jumping. His friends joke that he never seems happy unless he's risking his life in some crazy stunt, and Chance himself says that "nothing beats the thrill you get when you're facing possible death – what a rush!" Explain Chance's risky behavior, from the perspective of drive theory, arousal theory, and incentive theory.

2. At a bakery one day, you overhear a little girl ask her mother to buy her some cookies. "But Mommy," she says, "my tummy is telling me that it's hungry!" Discuss the biological mechanisms underlying hunger. Is the little girl correct in her assumption that her stomach is sending "eat" messages to her brain? What evidence is there that hunger is also a psychological experience?

3. Define the need for affiliation and contrast this motive with the need for intimacy. Examine personal (individual difference) and environmental factors that may influence the need for affiliation.

4. What evidence is there that the face communicates emotions in ways that are innate? In other words, are certain facial expressions inborn rather than learned?

5. Is cognition necessary for emotion?

TEST SOLUTIONS

Multiple-Choice Solutions

1. d (p. 377)
2. b (p. 377)
3. c (p. 378)
4. b (p. 378)
5. b (p. 379)
6. d (p. 380)
7. b (p. 381)
8. c (p. 381)
9. d (p. 382)
10. b (p. 383)

11. c (p. 385)
12. b (p. 387)
13. b (p. 390)
14. a (p. 391)
15. c (p. 392)
16. d (p. 394)
17. b (p. 395)
18. d (p. 395)
19. a (p. 395)
20. c (p. 396)

21. b (p. 400)
22. a (p. 400)
23. a (p. 402)
24. c (p. 403)
25. a (p. 404)
26. d (p. 408)
27. d (p. 408)
28. c (p. 410)
29. d (p. 410)
30. d (p. 411)

True-False Solutions

1. T (p. 377)
2. T (p. 377)
3. F (p. 379)
4. T (p. 381)
5. T (p. 391)

6. T (p. 394)
7. T (p. 396)
8. T (p. 400)
9. F (p. 407)
10. T (p. 408)

Key Concepts Matching Solutions

Exercise #1

1. e
2. j
3. h
4. i
5. c
6. f
7. d
8. a
9. g
10. b

Exercise #2

1. b
2. d
3. e
4. c
5. a

Essay Solutions

1. Well, Chance clearly likes to take risks and he seems to enjoy the rush of arousal associated with these daring activities. Drive theory would have a difficult time explaining Chance's behavior, since from that perspective we are motivated to reduce (and not increase) tension in order to return to a more pleasant, balanced state (pp. 377-378). Arousal theory does a much better job of explaining his behavior. According to this perspective, human beings are motivated to achieve and maintain an optimum level of arousal, and this optimum level may be different for different individuals. Thus, Chance just has a higher optimum level of arousal, and he needs to engage in constant risky behaviors to maintain this level (p. 377). Incentive theory would posit a different process still; according to this perspective, human behavior is motivated by external goals or forces. Chance perhaps has been rewarded in the past for his behavior (he earns the respect and admiration of his friends, for example), and he has come to value this reward, which now serves as an incentive that motivates his continued risky behavior (pp. 378-379).

2. Early researchers did believe exactly what the little girl believes; namely, that hunger was caused by sensations in the stomach. However, individuals who have had their stomachs removed for various reasons (and who therefore cannot experience stomach contractions or "hunger pangs") continue to feel hungry; therefore, the stomach alone cannot be responsible for hunger. Other biological mechanisms do appear to have a role in regulating hunger. For example, a complex biochemical system that includes the hypothalamus, nerves that run from the brainstem through the hypothalamus, and hormonal activities governed by the pancreas, liver, and intestines all appear to contribute to hunger. (pp. 380-381)

   Hunger also is governed by psychological processes. For example, hunger may increase or decrease as a function of such external factors as the smell, taste, and sight of food (the little girl may feel that her stomach is "hungry" due to the smell of the freshly baked cookies, or their mouth-watering appearance). Perhaps the time of day signals to her that it's snack time, or she sees other people eating the cookies. (p. 382)

3. The need for affiliation is the desire to establish and maintain social contacts, whereas the need for intimacy is the desire for close, intimate relationships characterized by self-disclosure. Both are belongingness motives (p. 390). There are definitely individual differences in the need for affiliation; people with a higher need are more gregarious and will expend greater effort maintaining social contact (e.g., send letters, make phone calls) than those with a lower need. In addition, however, we seem to have a "sociostat" or social thermometer that regulates our need for affiliation; after spending much time with others, most of us prefer reduced contact (pp. 390-391).

   Several environmental factors also influence affiliative needs. For example, people who are stressed are highly motivated to affiliate; we seek each other out in times of need in order to gain cognitive clarity (the information that others provide may help us cope with the situation). Others also provide emotional support, attention, and stimulation, and so we may seek them out when we feel a need for those experiences as well (p. 391).

4. There is some solid evidence that some emotional expressions are unlearned or innate. Cross-cultural research in which individuals from many different countries were shown pictures of faces with different emotional expressions reveals that people from different cultures can reliably identify certain emotions from facial expressions. No matter where in the world the subject was from there were able to identify six basic emotions: joy, surprise, anger, fear, disgust, and sadness. (pp. 398-400).

5. The debate continues to rage over whether cognition is necessary for emotion. On one hand, some researchers argue for the "primacy of affect." Zajonc, for example, suggests that people sometimes react with emotion instantly and without prior cognitive appraisal; we feel before we think. In support of his hypothesis, human infants demonstrate reflexive facial expressions of pain, joy, and so on to a stimulus before they have the neural capacity to actually make corresponding cognitive appraisals of the stimulus. In addition, animal research suggests that certain emotions (e.g., fear) are triggered instantly and do not involve the cerebral cortex (which means that the response does not necessarily involve an initial processing of information). On the other side of the debate, some researchers argue for the "primacy of cognition." Lazarus, for example, agrees that emotions may occur without awareness, but he maintains that it is impossible to have emotion without some kind of thought (although that thought may be unconscious and effortless). (pp. 405-407)

CHAPTER 11

SOCIAL AND CULTURAL INFLUENCES

CHAPTER OVERVIEW

This chapter explores some of the major topics in the field of social psychology. The first topic, social perception, concerns how individuals form impressions of others and how they make attributions, or draw conclusions, about the causes of other people's behavior. Next, the text examines several of the biases that cloud our judgment and prevent us from viewing other people accurately (e.g., self-serving biases, primacy effect, behavioral confirmation). The chapter then focuses on interpersonal attraction and two of the basic factors that influence our feelings of liking for others; namely, similarity and physical attractiveness. The next part of the chapter considers the topic of social influence. Conformity and obedience, and the variables that act to increase or decrease these types of social influence, are examined. The chapter then turns to a discussion of attitudes and the process of attitude change (called persuasion). The two cognitive routes to persuasion are discussed. This section concludes by considering the topic of self-persuasion (attitude change that is brought about by our own attitude-discrepant behavior). The next part of the chapter concerns group processes, including social facilitation and social loafing. The next section involves the topic of social relations, with a focus on aggression and altruism (prosocial or helping behavior). Each social behavior is defined, theories about its origin are presented, and the factors that increase or decrease the likelihood of its occurrence are identified and discussed. This chapter then expands upon the ways in which people are influenced by their own culture and the situations in which they find themselves. First, your author considers how the human population is distributed cross-culturally and examines how the implicit rules of conduct (called social norms) may differ across cultures. Then, the chapter discusses differences in the extent to which cultures value individualism or collectivism, and the origins of these orientations. The development and the personal (e.g., self-concept) and social consequences of these different cultural orientations also are addressed. The next part of the chapter concerns discrimination. This concept is defined, and its cognitive basis (including how stereotypes are formed and the process of social categorization) and motivational foundation (including realistic-conflict and social-identity theories of prejudice) are discussed. The chapter concludes with a consideration of racism in America.

CHAPTER OUTLINE

I. *What's Your Prediction* How Far Can People Be Pushed?

II. Social Perception

    A. Making Attributions
       1. Attribution theory

      2. The fundamental attribution error
      3. Attributions as cultural constructions
      4. Self-serving attributions

  B. Forming Impressions
      1. Cognitive-confirmation biases
      2. Behavioral-confirmation biases

  C. *The Process of Discovery* Robert Rosenthal

  D. Attraction
      1. Similarity and liking
      2. Physical attractiveness

III. Social Influence

  A. Social Influence as "Automatic"

  B. Conformity
      1. The early classics
      2. Majority influence
      3. Obedience to authority

  C. Attitude Change
      1. Persuasive communications
      2. Cognitive-dissonance theory

  D. *Psychology and Sports* Why Athletes Sometimes "Choke" Under Pressure

  E. Group Processes
      1. Social facilitation
      2. Social loafing

IV. Social Relations

  A. Aggression
      1. Biological roots
      2. Aversive stimulation
      3. Situational cues
         a. Weapons
         b. Media violence
      4. Deindividuation

  B. Altruism
      1. Bystander intervention

C. *The Process of Discovery* John M. Darley

V. Cross-Cultural Perspectives

    A. Cultural Diversity: A Fact of Life

    B. Individualism and Collectivism: A Tale of Two Cultural Worldviews
        1. Conceptions of the self

    C. *How To* Avoid Social Blunders When Traveling in Foreign Cultures

    D. *The Process of Discovery* Hazel Rose Markus

VI. Intergroup Discrimination

    A. Stereotypes

    B. Prejudice: The Motivational Roots
        1. Realistic conflict theory
        2. Social-identity theory

    C. Racism in America
        1. The problem
        2. The symptoms
        3. The treatment

VII. Thinking Like a Psychologist About Social and Cultural Influences

LEARNING OBJECTIVES

By the time you have read and reviewed this chapter, you should be able to:

1. Define social psychology and consider the topics of interest to social psychologists (p. 420).

2. Explain the concept of social perception (p. 420).

3. Define and provide an example of the fundamental attribution error (p. 421). Consider Gilbert's cognitive explanation for why people fall prey to the fundamental attribution error (pp. 421-422). Discuss just how "fundamental" this error is, using cross-cultural research to support your argument (p. 422).

4. Provide examples of and explain the purpose of self-serving attributions (p. 422).

5. Discuss the process of forming an impression of another person (p. 422). Consider the cognitive-confirmation and behavioral-confirmation biases that affect the process of impression formation (pp. 422-424).

6. Define the primacy effect and consider two reasons for the occurrence of this effect (p. 423).

7. Discuss the three-step process of behavioral confirmation or self-fulfilling prophecy (p. 424).

8. Explain the relationship between similarity and liking (p. 426). Define the mere-exposure effect (p. 426).

9. Consider the role that physical attractiveness plays in interpersonal attraction (pp. 426-427). Explain the components of physical attractiveness (e.g., average features) (p. 427).

10. Explain the ways in which social influence is an "automatic" process (p. 428).

11. Define conformity (p. 429) and explain the method and results of classic early studies of conformity (pp. 429-430). Distinguish between informational and normative social influence and consider the relation between these forms of social influence and conformity (p. 430).

12. Identify the situational factors (i.e., group size, presence of an ally, salience of social norms, culture) that increase or decrease majority influence (pp. 430-431).

13. Discuss Milgram's classic study on obedience – explain the procedure that he used and his results (p. 432). Consider three factors (i.e., authority status, victim proximity, situation) that affect obedience (p. 432).

14. Define the concept of attitude and consider ways to change attitudes (pp. 433-434). Compare the central and the peripheral route to persuasion (pp. 433-434).

15. Explain the concept of cognitive dissonance and how this state might lead to attitude change (pp. 434-435).

16. Explain the phenomenon of social facilitation and why the presence of others sometimes helps performance and sometimes causes it to decline. (pp. 436-438).

17. Define social loafing and explain why it occurs. (p. 438).

18. Define aggression (p. 439) and consider the biological (pp. 439-440) and situational (pp. 440-443) factors that influence aggression. Explain the frustration-aggression hypothesis (pp. 440-441). Consider how environmental (temperature, culture) conditions may influence aggression (p. 441). Examine the association between weapons and media violence and aggressive behavior (pp. 441-443).

19. Define altruism (p. 443). Consider the bystander effect (p. 444) and analyze the intervention process (pp. 444-446). Identify the factors that predict when helping behavior is most likely to occur (p. 446).

20. Consider the numerous ways in which all people are similar, and some of the ways in which each person is unique (p. 448).

21. Discuss how the world's population is distributed geographically (p. 448), and the ways in which social norms differ across cultures (pp. 448-449).

22. Distinguish between individualism and collectivism (p. 449), and discuss three key factors (i.e., complexity, affluence, and heterogeneity) that influence the development of these cultural orientations (p. 452).

23. Consider how the cultural orientations of individualism and collectivism can influence the ways in which people view themselves and others (p. 454).

24. Define the concept of stereotype and discuss how the formation of stereotypes involves two related processes (pp. 454-455). Explain how the process of social categorization contributes to the outgroup-homogeneity bias (p. 455). Consider whether stereotypes can be automatically activated (p. 455).

25. Describe the two major motivational theories of prejudice, realistic conflict theory and social identity theory. (pp. 456-458).

26. Define racism (p. 458) and consider the methods psychologists use to detect racist beliefs (pp. 458-461).

KEY TERMS

The following key terms and concepts are featured in this chapter and are important for you to know. Write out definitions of each term and check your answers with the definitions in the text on the pages listed.

Social psychology (p. 420)
Social perception (p. 420)
Attribution theory (p. 420)
Fundamental attribution error (p. 421)
Primacy effect (p. 423)
Mere-exposure effect (p. 426)
Conformity (p. 429)
Informational influence (p. 430)
Normative influence (p. 430)
Attitude (p. 433)

Central route to persuasion (p. 433)
Peripheral route to persuasion (p. 433)
Cognitive dissonance (p. 434)
Social facilitation (p. 438)
Social loafing (p. 438)
Aggression (p. 438)
Frustration-aggression hypothesis (p. 441)
Altruism (p. 443)
Bystander effect (p. 444)
Diffusion of responsibility (p. 446)
Social norms (p. 449)
Individualism (p. 449)
Collectivism (p. 449)
Discrimination (p. 454)
Stereotype (p. 454)
Social categorization (p. 455)
Outgroup-homogeneity bias (p. 455)
Prejudice (p. 457)
Realistic-conflict theory (p. 457)
Ingroup favoritism (p. 457)
Social-identity theory (p. 457)
Racism (p. 458)
Implicit Association Test (IAT) (p. 460)

TEST QUESTIONS

Multiple-Choice Questions

Circle the correct choice for each question and compare your answers with those at the end of the Study Guide chapter.

1. _____ is the study of how individuals come to understand and evaluate other people.
   a. Social cognition
   b. Social perception
   c. Self-perception
   d. Self-cognition

2. The fundamental attribution error is the tendency to overattribute a person's behavior to _____ causes and to underestimate the importance of _____ causes.
   a. personal; situational
   b. internal; personal
   c. stimulus; situational
   d. distinctive; consistent

3. During a research meeting, a professor praises a student at great length. Which of the following conclusions that you might draw illustrates the fundamental attribution error?
    a. "The professor behaved that way because she believes that student is brilliant."
    b. "The professor behaved that way because the student sucked up to her."
    c. "The professor behaved that way because the student truly did deserve praise."
    d. "The professor behaved that way because other professors told her to be nice to students."

4. You notice your friend Harold helping an elderly woman load groceries into her car. According to the two-step attribution process outlined by social psychologists Gilbert and Malone (1995), which of the following inferences will you <u>first</u> make when trying to understand the causes of Harold's behavior?
    a. "Harold helped the woman because he is a really kind person."
    b. "Harold helped the woman because he is really kind and also because the woman asked him for assistance."
    c. "Harold helped the woman because she asked him for assistance."
    d. "There is no way to tell why Harold helped the woman."

5. A _____ effect occurs when early information about a person has a stronger impact on perceivers' impressions than later information.
    a. recency
    b. primacy
    c. situational
    d. dispositional

6. Nicole sees the same dog every day on her way to work. Although she initially paid little attention to him, she finds that she misses the dog when his owners move away. Nicole's feelings for the dog reflect the _____.
    ·a. bias for beauty
    b. fundamental attribution error
    c. mere exposure effect
    d. interpersonal attraction effect

7. Based on research examining physical attractiveness, which one of the following men will be rated as most attractive?
    a. Brian, who has extremely unusual, distinctive features
    b. Alan, who has average features
    c. Tom, who has features that resemble a famous celebrity
    d. Glen, who has childlike features

8. Irena usually does not drink. However, when she is at a campus party, she notices that all her friends seem to be drinking. As a result, she begins to drink. Irena's behavior illustrates
   a. conformity.
   b. pressure.
   c. dissonance.
   d. obedience.

9. North is debating between signing up for math or geology. His sister tells him, "Oh, take the math course. The professors in the math department are pretty good." North knows that his sister has taken both math and geology courses, and so he decides to follow her advice and sign up for math. North's decision is based upon _____.
   a. normative social influence
   b. informational social influence
   c. obedience
   d. social pressure

10. People sometimes conform to normative social influence because _____.
    a. they believe that others have information that they themselves lack
    b. they fear the social rejection that might follow nonconforming behavior
    c. they are high self-monitors
    d. they are immoral

11. People sometimes conform to informational social influence because _____.
    a. they assume that the majority is correct
    b. past experience has shown them that nonconformity will be punished by other group members
    c. they believe that they can sway the opinions of group members later
    d. they fear social rejection

12. A factor that influences conformity is
    a. the size of the majority.
    b. whether the dissenter has an ally.
    c. the salience of group norms.
    d. All of the above

13. Ed is watching a commercial on television for a diet soda. He sees handsome men and beautiful women drinking the soda and having a fun time together. Ed decides to buy some of that diet soda the next time he goes shopping. Ed has been persuaded via the _____.
    a. central route
    b. attitude route
    c. peripheral route
    d. dissonance route

14. The _____ route to persuasion takes place when people think carefully about the content of the persuasive message.
    a. central
    b. medium
    c. peripheral
    d. cognitive

15. Cognitive dissonance is a state of _____.
    a. physical illness
    b. mental disorder
    c. psychological tension
    d. brain activity

16. Research on the social facilitation effect demonstrates that higher arousal leads to _____ performance when tasks are difficult and _____ performance when tasks are easy or well-learned.
    a. decreased; increased
    b. increased; decreased
    c. decreased; decreased
    d. increased; increased

17. The decrease in individual effort that occurs when people engage in shared group activity is called _____.
    a. deindividuation
    b. social facilitation
    c. laziness
    d. social loafing

18. Which of the following factors are implicated in producing aggression?
    a. temperature
    b. the presence of a weapon
    c. media violence
    d. All of the above

19. John is walking to work one day when he sees an elderly man stumble and fall to the sidewalk. There are many other people present, but no one stops to help. John also does not stop. John's behavior may reflect _____.
    a. prosocial behavior
    b. aggression
    c. diffusion of responsibility
    d. egocentricity

20. Individualistic cultures value traits associated with
    a. cooperation.
    b. independence.
    c. social harmony.
    d. interdependence.

21. A collectivist culture tends to value characteristics and behaviors associated with
    a. autonomy.
    b. self-reliance.
    c. cooperation.
    d. independence.

22. Some psychologists speculate that there are a number of key factors that influence a culture's orientation toward individualism or collectivism, including
    a complexity.
    b affluence.
    c heterogeneity.
    d All of the above

23. Jane is from an individualistic culture; Bibiana is from a collectivist culture. When asked, Jane is likely to describe herself as _____ and Bibiana is likely to describe herself as _____.
    a. shy; intelligent
    b. friendly; a college student
    c. a college student; shy
    d. a woman; a banker

24. Behavior that is directed against persons because of their group membership is called
    a. discrimination.
    b. prejudice.
    c. stereotyping.
    d. All of the above

25. Which one of the following statements about stereotyping is accurate?
    a. A stereotype is an overt hostile action directed against someone because of his or her group membership.
    b. Social categorization is an unnatural and maladaptive process.
    c. Stereotypes are always negative.
    d. Stereotypes can be brought to mind automatically.

26. Lori is homosexual and she views her homosexual friends as distinct and unique individuals. However, she assumes that all heterosexuals are the same. Lori's thinking reflects the _____.
    a. ingroup heterogeneity bias
    b. outgroup-homogeneity bias
    c. ingroup-outgroup bias
    d. person positivity bias

27. We are most likely to rely on stereotypes when forming an impression of another person when we are _____.
    a. busy and distracted
    b. mentally tired
    c. pressed for time
    d. All of the above

28. Tom learns that Sally Jones is the name of the new company president. His first response to this information is, "Oh great, a woman president. I'm going to hate working for her. I don't like her already. Why can't the company hire a man?" Tom's response reflects
    a. schemas.
    b. discrimination.
    c. stereotypes.
    d. prejudice.

29. The view that prejudice is the result of direct competition between groups over valued but limited resources is called _____.
    a. competition theory
    b. social deprivation theory
    c. realistic-conflict theory
    · d. social-identity theory

30. Social–Identity theory predicts that threats to one's self-esteem will
    a. increase the need to exhibit prejudice.
    b. decrease the need to exhibit prejudice.
    c. increase our pride in past accomplishments.
    d. decrease our pride in past accomplishments.

True-False Questions

Indicate which of the following statements are true or false, and compare your answers with those at the end of the chapter.

T F   1. The fundamental attribution error occurs mostly in Western cultures.

T F   2. Once people form an impression, they often interpret later information in light of that first impression.

T F   3. Attitude-discrepant behavior can produce attitude change.

T F   4. On easy tasks, the presence of others does not affect our performance.

T F   5. Aggression is not subject to biological influences.

T F   6. There are tremendous variations in the social norms that characterize different cultures.

T F   7. There appears to be a close link between cultural orientation and the self-concept.

T F   8. Stereotypes can be activated without our awareness.

T F   9. Expressions of prejudice may enhance self-esteem in certain circumstances.

T F   10. Stereotypes can be assessed only with direct behavioral tests.

Key Concepts Matching Exercises

Exercise #1: Two Routes to Persuasion

Indicate which of the items listed on the right will induce attitude change via the central route or the peripheral route.

_____ 1. Central Route

_____ 2. Peripheral Route

a. attractiveness of source

b. quality of message arguments

c. strength of message arguments

d. emotional response by target audience

e. high involvement by target audience

f. high ability to think critically about message by target audience

g. reaction of others to message

Exercise #2: The Helping Decision Tree

Latané and Darley provided a step-by-step analysis of the decision-making process that bystanders go through when faced with an emergency situation. Match the statements on the right with the appropriate step in that process.

_____ Step 1

_____ Step 2

_____ Step 3

_____ Step 4

_____ Step 5

a. "That's it, I've decided – I'm going to help that kid."

b. "Hey, what was that? I think I heard a scream."

c. "I wonder why no one else is helping? Maybe I should be the one to help."

d. "Here I come, kid – give me your hand and I'll pull you up!"

e. "Oh my gosh, that kid needs help!"

Exercise #3: Social and Cultural Groups

Match the key terms on the left with the definitions on the right.

_____ 1. Social norms

_____ 2. Individualism

_____ 3. Collectivism

_____ 4. Social-identity theory

_____ 5. Discrimination

_____ 6. Realistic-conflict theory

_____ 7. Stereotype

_____ 8. Prejudice

_____ 9. Outgroup-homogeneity bias

a. "I refuse to rent rooms to unmarried couples."

b. "It makes me feel better to hate you and your kind."

c. "They're all the same, every last one of them."

d. "Group harmony is more important than individual goals."

e. the implicit rules that govern behavior in a particular culture

f. "I don't like my new neighbor. He's one of them, and I don't like his kind of people."

g. the notion that prejudice stems from competition over limited resources

h. beliefs about the characteristics of the members of particular social groups

i. "Personal glory is more important than group allegiance."

Essay Questions

Write out answers to the following brief essay questions. Compare your responses with the sample answers at the end of the Study Guide chapter.

1. Define and give an example of the fundamental attribution error. What might explain why this error occurs? Exactly how "fundamental" is the fundamental attribution error?

2. What is the primacy effect? What two reasons explain why this effect occurs?

3. Bud is out walking his dog when he sees a woman on rollerblades lose her footing and fall to the ground. List the five decision-making points that Bud must cognitively traverse in determining whether to help the fallen rollerblader. Assuming that other people are present, how might this affect whether Bud helps the woman?

4. List and describe the three key factors that determine whether a culture is individualistic or collectivistic in orientation.

5. What is a stereotype? In what way is stereotyping an adaptive or useful process? In what way is it a maladaptive process?

TEST SOLUTIONS

Multiple-Choice Solutions

1. b (p. 420)
2. a (p. 421)
3. a (p. 421)
4. a (pp. 421-422)
5. b (p. 423)
6. c (p. 426)
7. b (p. 427)
8. a (p. 429)
9. b (p. 430)
10. b (p. 430)

11. a (p. 430)
12. d (p. 431)
13. c (p. 433)
14. a (p. 433)
15. c (p. 435)
16. a (pp. 437-438)
17. d (p. 438)
18. d (pp. 441-442)
19. c (p. 446)
20. b (p. 449)

21. c (p. 449)
22. d (p. 452)
23. b (p. 454)
24. a (p. 454)
25. d (pp. 454-455)
26. b (p. 455)
27. d (pp. 455-456)
28. d (p. 456)
29. c (p. 456)
30. a (p. 458)

True-False Solutions

1. T (p. 422)
2. T (p. 423)
3. T (p. 435)
4. F (pp. 437-438)
5. F (pp. 439-440)

6. T (p. 449)
7. T (p. 454)
8. T (p. 455)
9. T (p. 458)
10. F (p. 459)

Key Concepts Matching Solutions

Exercise #1

1. b, c, e, f
2. a, d, g

Exercise #2

1. b
2. e
3. c
4. a
5. d

Exercise #3

1. e
2. i
3. d
4. b
5. a
6. g
7. h
8. f
9. c

Essay Solutions

1. The fundamental attribution error is the tendency to overattribute other people's behavior to personal causes while at the same time failing to recognize the importance of situational causes (p. 421). An example might be when you assume that your roommate's lateness in paying his or her share of the rent is due to his or her innate stinginess and irresponsibility rather than to the fact that he or she had other, more pressing financial concerns.

    The fundamental attribution error might occur as a result of the basic two-step process that perceivers follow when making an attribution. Gilbert argues, for example, that perceivers first identify the behavior and then make an immediate personal attribution, and then correct or adjust this personal attribution by taking situational causes into account. The first step is simple and automatic; the second requires attention, thought, and effort. Anything that prevents attention or impedes thought will prevent the second step from occurring, and perceivers will rely on the initial personal attribution (pp. 421-422).

    The fundamental attribution error is not as fundamental as theorists originally assumed. Specifically, it appears to occur or be most pervasive in cultures that emphasize the person over the situation (i.e., that view individuals as autonomous and responsible for their own behaviors). Non-Western cultures that commonly take a more holistic, collective view that focuses on the relationship between individuals and their social roles are less prone to the fundamental attribution error (p. 422).

2. The primacy effect refers to the finding that people are influenced more by information that they receive early in an interaction than by information that appears later (p. 422). This effect occurs for two reasons. First, we become less attentive to later behavioral evidence once we have already formed an impression (perhaps out of fatigue or boredom); if we are alert and/or motivated, this bias is diminished. Second, once we form an impression, we interpret subsequent information in light of that initial impression (this is called the change-of-meaning hypothesis); so any new information merely bolsters the first impression, because it is interpreted in line with that impression (p. 423).

3. According to Latané and Darley's (1970) analysis of the decision-making process in emergency situations, Bud must (1) notice the incident, (2) interpret the incident as an emergency, (3) take responsibility for helping the fallen rollerblader, (4) decide to intervene, and (5) act on his decision. The presence of others can inhibit helping at each of these five stages. For example, if he sees the woman fall and also sees that others are not reacting, he may interpret the incident as a non-emergency (step 2). In addition, the presence of others may lead to diffusion of responsibility, which is the belief that others will intervene; assuming that others will help, he may not take responsibility (step 3). (pp. 444-446)

4. Triandis (1995) suggests that there are three key factors that determine whether a culture is relatively collectivistic or individualistic in orientation. The first is the complexity of a society. Highly complex, industrialized cultures contain more groups with which individual members can identity (family, hometown, church, school, occupation, political party, etc.). This results in less loyalty to any one group and a greater focus on personal rather than collective goals and concerns. The second factor is the affluence of the society. Individuals in wealthy cultures are more mobile and socially independent than individuals who reside in less affluent cultures; consequently, they are also more independent and less interdependent in orientation. The third factor is heterogeneity. Societies that are heterogeneous (contain many diverse members) tend to be more permissive of difference or dissent, which allows for greater individualism. (p. 452)

5. A stereotype is a belief that associates a whole group of people with certain traits (p. 454). The process of stereotyping – social categorization – is to some extent adaptive; specifically, stereotypes allow us to make judgments about someone quickly and easily without taking the time to gather individualized information. The problem, of course (and here's where stereotyping can get us into trouble), is that these quick and easy judgments may be grossly inaccurate (p. 455).

CHAPTER 12

PERSONALITY

CHAPTER OVERVIEW

In contrast to the last chapter, which focused upon social and cultural influences, this chapter explores personality, defined as an individual's distinct and enduring pattern of thoughts, feelings, motives, and behaviors. Four major approaches to personality are considered. First, the chapter examines Freudian psychoanalysis, including work by Charcot and Breuer that shaped Freud's theory of personality, the division of personality into id, ego, and superego structural components, the psychosexual stages of development that each of us passes through as our personalities form and take shape, and the dynamics involved in the use of defense mechanisms to guard against anxiety. The ways in which subsequent generations of psychoanalytic theorists have altered classic Freudian theory are discussed, as are the major limitations and legacies of psychoanalysis. Second, the cognitive social-learning approach to personality is discussed, including how Watson and Skinner applied principles of learning to the study of personality; how observational or social learning (modeling), locus of control, and self-efficacy affect behavior; and the methods used by this approach to assess personality. Third, the basic principles of the humanistic approach to personality are considered, as well as the tenets of the theories of Rogers (e.g., self-actualization, the need for positive regard, unconditional positive regard, conditional positive regard) and Maslow (e.g., self-actualization, peak experiences). The limitations and influence of humanistic personality theory are discussed. The fourth approach that is considered in this chapter is the trait approach. Early work on the basic units of personality conducted by Allport and Cattell is discussed, and the five-factor model of personality is presented. Assessment devices, the biological basis of various traits, and the trait dimension of introversion and extraversion are considered, and the debate about the existence of traits is explored.

CHAPTER OUTLINE

I. *What's Your Prediction* How Stable Is Personality?

II. Psychoanalysis

    A. The Birth of Psychoanalysis

    B. Freud's Theory of Personality
        1. The unconscious
        2. The structure of personality
        3. Psychosexual development
        4. The dynamics of personality

C. Freud's Legacy
    1. Neo-Freudian theorists
    2. Projective personality tests
    3. Current perspectives on psychoanalysis

III. The Cognitive Social-Learning Approach

    A. Principles of Learning and Behavior

    B. Social-Learning Theory
        1. Locus of control
        2. Self-efficacy

    C. Perspectives on Cognitive Social-Learning Theory

IV. The Humanistic Approach

    A. Carl Rogers
        1. Rogers's theory
        2. Self-esteem

    B. Abraham Maslow
        1. Maslow's theory
        2. The state of self-actualization

    C. Perspectives on the Humanistic Approach

V. The Trait Approach

    A. The Building Blocks of Personality

    B. Construction of Multitrait Inventories

    C. Biological Roots of Personality

    D. Introversion and Extraversion

    E. Perspectives: Do Traits Exist?

    F. *The Process of Discovery* Jerome Kagan

    G. *Psychology and Business* Use of Personality Tests in the Workplace

VI. Thinking Like a Psychologist About Personality

LEARNING OBJECTIVES

By the time you have read and reviewed this chapter, you should be able to:

1. Define the concept of personality (p. 468) and list and describe the four major approaches to personality (p. 469).

2. Describe how Freud's early work with the neurologist Jean Charcot and with the physician Josef Breuer contributed to his notion of psychoanalysis (pp. 469-470).

3. Describe the phenomenon of transference (p. 470). Describe the techniques and phenomena of psychoanalysis (e.g., free association, resistance) (p. 470).

4. Explain Freud's division of the mind and consider what is contained in each portion of the human mind (pp. 470-471). Distinguish between the life and death instincts (p. 471).

5. Outline the structure of personality and describe the three parts of personality (p. 471).

6. Describe Freud's two conclusions about personality development (p. 472) and outline the five psychosexual stages of personality development (pp. 472-473). Consider the concept of fixation and the three personality types that reflect fixation (p. 473).

7. List and describe six common defense mechanisms (pp. 474-475).

8. Discuss how the theories of the neo-Freudians (Jung, Adler, Fromm, Horney) and ego psychologists (A. Freud, Hartmann, Rapaport, Erikson, White, etc.) were similar to and different from classic Freudian theory (pp. 475-476).

9. Describe the purpose of projective tests (p. 476). Explain the procedures used in the Rorschach and Thematic Apperception Test (TAT) (pp. 476-478).

10. Consider three major criticisms of psychoanalysis (pp. 478-479). Explore the continuing contributions of Freudian theory (pp. 479-480).

11. Describe the cognitive social-learning approach to personality (p. 480). Describe the five basic principles of learning (classical conditioning, operant conditioning, stimulus generalization, discrimination, and extinction) (p. 481). Explain Skinner's definition of personality (p. 482).

12. Explain how Bandura and Rotter expanded behaviorism to better account for personality processes (p. 482). Describe how modeling (social learning) and expectancies and values can shape personality (p. 482).

13. Discuss Mischel's "cognitive" social-learning theory and outline the five "person variables" that determine how we interact with our environment (pp. 482-483).

14. Define locus of control and explain how it influences behavior (p. 483). Consider whether having an internal locus of control is always adaptive (p. 484).

15. Define self-efficacy, consider sources of self-efficacy, and describe the consequences of self-efficacy (pp. 484-485).

16. Explain the concept of reciprocal determinism (p. 485) and discuss the methods used by cognitive social-learning theorists to assess personality (p. 485).

17. List and describe the four basic principles of the humanistic theory of personality (p. 486).

18. Describe Rogers's theory of personality and explain the need for self-actualization and the need for positive regard (p. 486). Compare unconditional positive regard and conditional positive regard (p. 486).

19. Explain how the self-concept (self-schemas, self-esteem, self-discrepancies) may affect our emotional state (pp. 487-489).

20. Describe Maslow's theory of personality (pp. 489-490). Consider the state of self-actualization and how this is related to peak experiences (p. 490).

21. Consider the limitations and the legacies of the humanistic approach (p. 492).

22. Explore the basic assumption of the trait approach to personality (p. 493) and list and describe the "big five" factors of personality (p. 493).

23. Describe multitrait inventories of personality (p. 494). Consider the development of the MMPI (pp. 494-496).

24. Discuss research findings on the biological basis of personality (pp. 496-497).

25. Compare introversion and extraversion (p. 498). Consider the biological basis for these traits, and discuss the relation between these traits and other personality characteristics (pp. 498-500).

26. Consider Mischel's critique of the trait approach to personality (p. 502). Discuss Epstein's response (p. 502). Explore the interaction between our traits and the situations in which we find ourselves (p. 502). Consider whether personality demonstrates stability over time (pp. 503-504).

27. Discuss the use of personality tests for employment purposes (p. 503).

KEY TERMS

The following key terms and concepts are featured in this chapter and are important for you to know. Write out definitions of each term and check your answers with the definitions in the text on the pages listed.

Personality (p. 468)
Psychoanalysis (p. 471)
Id (p. 471)
Pleasure principle (p. 471)
Superego (p. 471)
Ego (p. 471)
Reality principle (p. 471)
Psychosexual stages (p. 472)
Oedipus complex (p. 472)
Identification (p. 472)
Fixation (p. 473)
Defense mechanisms (p. 474)
Repression (p. 474)
Denial (p. 475)
Projection (p. 475)
Reaction formation (p. 475)
Rationalization (p. 475)
Sublimation (p. 475)
Collective unconscious (p. 475)
Projective tests (p. 476)
Rorschach (p. 476)
Thematic Apperception Test (TAT) (p. 477)
Cognitive social-learning theory (p. 480)
Modeling (p. 482)
Locus of control (p. 483)
Self-efficacy (p. 484)
Reciprocal determinism (p. 485)
Humanistic theory (p. 486)
Unconditional positive regard (p. 486)
Conditional positive regard (p. 486)
Self-schemas (p. 487)
Self-esteem (p. 487)
Self-discrepancy theory (p. 488)
Self-actualization (p. 488)
Peak experience (p. 490)
Trait (p. 493)

TEST QUESTIONS

Multiple-Choice Questions

Circle the correct choice for each question and compare your answers with those at the end of the Study Guide chapter.

1. The concept of "personality" refers to an individual's distinct pattern of _____.
   a. thoughts and feelings
   b. motives and values
   c. behaviors
   d. All of the above

2. Dr. S. has been seeing a client for two years. During this time, her client has become quite attached to her, and in fact is growing increasingly affectionate in their sessions. Dr. S. suspects that she is not the real target of her client's affection, and that his behavior may demonstrate
   a. free association.
   b. transference.
   c. resistance.
   d. hysteria.

3. Against her wishes, Andrea's parents have signed her up for psychoanalysis. She dislikes her therapy and constantly makes up excuses not to attend the sessions. When she does attend, she frequently is distracted and prone to lose her train of thought. Andrea may be experiencing _____.
   a. transference
   b. free association
   c. resistance
   d. insight

4. Conscious is to "tip of the iceberg" as unconscious is to _____.
   a. ice cube
   b. icicle
   c. ocean
   d. blue whale

5. The life instincts include _____.
    a. the need for food
    b. the need for sex
    c. the need for air
    d. All of the above

6. Which of the following statements illustrates the role of the superego?
    a. "You really shouldn't do that. Nice people don't act that way."
    b. "I want it all, and I want it now!"
    c. "Can't we all just be reasonable? I'm sure we can work out a compromise."
    d. All of the above

7. Which of the following statements illustrates the role of the ego?
    a. "You really shouldn't do that. Nice people don't act that way."
    b. "I want it all, and I want it now!"
    c. "Can't we all just be reasonable? I'm sure we can work out a compromise."
    d. All of the above

8. Weaning is to oral stage as _____ is to anal stage.
    a. Oedipal complex
    b. toilet training
    c. sexual attraction
    d. envy

9. Brant is an overweight man who eats, drinks, and smokes too much. He chews on pencils and his fingernails, and spends hours talking on the phone with friends and family. He also tends to be demanding and dependent in his relations with others. Freud might argue that Brant has a(n) _____ personality.
    a. oral
    b. anal
    c. phallic
    d. expulsive

10. Gloria is described by others as "uptight" and "rigid." She gets extremely upset when she is faced with events that are beyond her control, and insists on following an organized protocol or plan for each day of the week. She is stubborn and controlling in her relations with others. Freud would probably describe Gloria as having a(n) _____ personality.
    a. oral
    b. anal-retentive
    c. anal-expulsive
    d. phallic

11. When Art was a small child, his parents adopted a little girl. Art promptly "forgot" that he was potty-trained and began urinating in the closet. As an adult, Art cannot remember that he did this, despite what his parents tell him. This is an example of _____.
    a. projection
    b. reaction formation
    c. rationalization
    d. repression

12. A person who channels his or her aggressive impulses into a medical career has experienced _____.
    a. projection
    b. reaction formation
    c. sublimation
    d. repression

13. "Well, I never really wanted that class, anyway. It's just as well that it was full. I heard the professor was unfair and the book was way too hard. I'll be better off with this other class." This is an example of
    a. rationalization.
    b. sublimation.
    c. reaction formation.
    d. projection.

14. According to Jung, the collective unconscious
    a. is inherited.
    b. consists of universal symbols and memories from the ancestral past.
    c. explains why common themes occur in cultural myths and legends around the world.
    d. All of the above

15. Jung and Adler criticized Freudian theory as relying too heavily upon _____.
    a. consciousness
    b. sexuality
    c. tension
    d. irrationality

16. Scott volunteered for a psychology study. Upon arrival at the lab, he is asked to complete a series of statements (for example, "When I think about my father, I …"). The psychologist then examines Scott's responses for a pattern. Scott has taken a _____.
    a. personality test
    b. multiphasic inventory
    c. projective test
    d. rejective test

17. Both the Rorschach and the TAT have been criticized for _____.
    a. lacking reliability and validity
    b. lacking subjectivity
    c. being too objective
    d. All of the above

18. The "person variables" that are considered important by cognitive social-learning theorists include
    a. mental and physical competencies.
    b. expectancies.
    c. subjective values.
    d. All of the above

19. The person variable called _____ encompasses the ability to set goals, monitor and evaluate our progress, plan for the future, and delay our short-term needs for gratification.
    a. self-regulatory systems
    b. expectancies
    c. competencies
    d. subjective values

20. According to the social-learning approach to personality, behavior is influenced by _____.
    a. unconscious drives
    b. only actual reinforcements
    c. observation and imitation
    d. All of the above

21. Lucia believes that she is in charge of her own destiny. She takes difficult classes and accepts responsibility for her successes and failures. Rowena is just the opposite. She attributes her successes to luck and her failures to misfortune or her professor's whim. Lucia has an _____ locus of control; Rowena has an _____ locus of control.
    a. internal; internal
    b. internal; external
    c. external; external
    d. external; internal

22. According to Rogers's humanistic theory, all people are motivated by a need for
    a. self-actualization.
    b. positive regard.
    c. inner wisdom.
    d. a and b

23. Carl has recently decided to leave medical school and pursue a career as an artist. His parents, however, are deeply disappointed with his decision. Carl is experiencing _____ from his parents.
    a. positive regard
    b. unconditional positive regard
    c. conditional positive regard
    d. negative regard

24. Research suggests that when our self-concept does not match our self-guides, we may experience which of the following?
    a. lowered self-esteem
    b. negative emotions
    c. depression
    d. All of the above

25. Maslow believed that self-actualized people are
    a. spontaneous.
    b. independent.
    c. creative.
    d. All of the above

26. A peak experience is defined as a moment of _____.
    a. self-actualization
    b. positive regard
    c. unconditional love
    d. being in the zone

27. Which of the following factors are members of the "big five?"
    a. neuroticism, openness, and extraversion
    b. conscientiousness, anxiety, and psychoticism
    c. introversion, sensation seeking, and neuroticism
    d. emotionality, agreeableness, and shyness

28. Lisa is good-natured, soft-hearted, courteous, and sympathetic. She probably would score high on the factor called _____.
    a. neuroticism
    b. extraversion
    c. agreeableness
    d. conscientiousness

29. Research suggests which of the following about introversion and extraversion?
    a. Introverts are less aroused by social stimulation than are extraverts.
    b. Extraverts are more sensation-seeking than are introverts.
    c. Introversion has a biological basis, whereas extraversion does not.
    d. Extraverts are more easily aroused by caffeine and other "uppers" than are introverts.

30. Traits are expressed
    a. only in relevant situations.
    b. only in situations that do not constrain our behavior.
    c. Both of the above
    d. None of the above

True-False Questions

Indicate which of the following statements are true or false, and compare your answers with those at the end of the chapter.

T F   1. Personality does not appear to be highly stable over time.

T F   2. Freudian psychoanalysis and theory focuses on the events and traumas of early childhood.

T F   3. Neo-Freudian theorists disagreed with Freud over the primacy of sex as a driving force in personality development.

T F   4. The TAT and the Rorschach test have high validity and reliability.

T F   5. The cognitive social-learning approach views personality as determined by actual reinforcement contingencies.

T F   6. Research suggests that it is always better to have an internal locus of control.

T F   7. The humanistic theory of personality emphasizes the past rather than the present, and biological determinism rather than choice and free will.

T F   8. Most adults will reach a state of self-actualization.

T F   9. Empirical evidence generally supports the five-factor model of personality.

T F   10. Research suggests that personality characteristics are to some extent, biologically determined.

Key Concepts Matching Exercises

Exercise #1: Personality

Match the key terms on the left with the definitions on the right.

_____ 1. Personality

_____ 2. Psychoanalysis

_____ 3. Id

_____ 4. Pleasure principle

_____ 5. Superego

_____ 6. Ego

_____ 7. Reality principle

_____ 8. Defense mechanisms

_____ 9. Collective unconscious

_____ 10. Rorschach

_____ 11. TAT

_____ 12. Cognitive social-learning theory

_____ 13. Self-efficacy

_____ 14. Humanistic theory

_____ 15. Unconditional positive regard

_____ 16. Conditional positive regard

_____ 17. Self-actualization

_____ 18. Trait

a. controlled by the unconscious, these reduce anxiety by distorting or denying reality

b. the personality approach that focuses on social learning, cognitive factors, and the person-situation interaction

c. a person's distinct and stable pattern of thoughts, feelings, motives, and behavior

d. associated with Jung, this is a memory bank that contains images from our evolutionary past

e. a stable predisposition to behave in a particular way

f. "I'll love you as long as you continue to be the kind of person I want you to be."

g. "Me, me, me. I want instant gratification, and make it snappy!"

h. the ego's capacity to delay gratification

i. the inkblot test

j. the drive for immediate gratification of desires

k. the personality approach that focuses on the self, subjective experience, and self-actualization

l. "I think that I can do the task and achieve the goal."

m. the "do"s and "don'ts" of personality

n. "Be all that you can be."

o. ambiguous pictures onto which people project their personalities

p. the part of personality that mediates the conflict between the id and the superego

q. the theory of personality that is associated with Freud

r. "I'll love you no matter what."

Exercise #2: Defense mechanisms

Match the statements on the right with the appropriate defense mechanism.

_____ 1. Repression

a. "I really do love you, sis! I enjoy spending time at home helping you. I'm not at all resentful of the fact that I've had to quit my job to help care for you, honest!"

_____ 2. Denial

b. "My painting really lets me express my creative urges. I enjoy the way the colors seem to melt and flow onto the canvas."

_____ 3. Projection

c. "What do you mean? My son never told me that he was gay. You must be insane."

_____ 4. Reaction formation

d. "I really don't care if he heard me talking about him. I mean, it's not like I said anything untrue, and besides, I've never really liked him that much anyway."

_____ 5. Rationalization

e. "I have very little memory of the time I fooled around with my best friend's partner in high school."

_____ 6. Sublimation

f. "I just know that my neighbor dislikes me. I've never done anything to her, but she always acts like she hates me."

Essay Questions

Write out answers to the following brief essay questions. Compare your responses with the sample answers at the end of the Study Guide chapter.

1. Describe one of the first three stages of personality development in Freud's theory. Be sure to discuss the ages, focus of energy, and the crisis of this stage, how resolution is achieved, and personality disorders associated with this stage. THEN give an example (and be specific) of a person you know who appears to have one of these disorders (do not use names if you use someone other than yourself!).

2. What are the three major criticisms of classic Freudian theory? Discuss some enduring legacies of Freudian theory as well.

3. Explain the concept of locus of control. What is the difference between an internal and an external locus of control? What are the consequences of having an internal as opposed to an external locus of control? Is an internal locus always adaptive?

4. Describe the two needs that all humans have, according to Rogers. What happens when these needs conflict with one another? Describe the consequences of experiencing conditional positive regard.

5. Discuss evidence that personality may be influenced by genetic and other biological factors.

TEST SOLUTIONS

Multiple-Choice Solutions

1. d (p. 468)	11. d (p. 474)	21. b (p. 483)
2. b (p. 470)	12. c (p. 474)	22. d (p. 486)
3. c (p. 470)	13. a (p. 475)	23. c (p. 486)
4. c (p. 470)	14. d (p. 475)	24. d (p. 489)
5. d (p. 471)	15. b (p. 475)	25. d (p. 490)
6. a (p. 471)	16. c (p. 476)	26. a (p. 490)
7. c (p. 471)	17. a (p. 478)	27. a (p. 493)
8. b (p. 472)	18. d (pp. 482-483)	28. c (p. 493)
9. a (p. 473)	19. a (p. 483)	29. b (p. 499)
10. b (p. 473)	20. c (p. 482)	30. c (p. 502)

True-False Solutions

1. F (p. 468)	6. F (p. 484)
2. T (p. 470)	7. F (p. 486)
3. T (p. 475)	8. F (p. 490)
4. F (p. 477)	9. T (p. 493)
5. F (p. 482)	10. T (p. 497)

Key Concepts Matching Solutions

Exercise #1

1. c	10. i
2. q	11. o
3. g	12. b
4. j	13. l
5. m	14. k
6. p	15. r
7. h	16. f
8. a	17. n
9. d	18. e

Exercise #2

1. e
2. c
3. f
4. a
5. d
6. b

Essay Solutions

1. You should describe one of the following (pp. 472-473):

   Oral stage: This occurs during the first year of life, and the mouth is the focus of energy or attention. The crisis is weaning, which is resolved when the baby is weaned successfully. If the child receives too much or too little oral stimulation, he or she is said to be fixated at the oral stage of development. Someone with an oral personality (fixated at this stage) might focus a lot of energy on oral activities (eating, smoking, drinking, biting nails or pens, chewing gum, talking) and also might seek symbolic forms of oral gratification by becoming passive, dependent, and demanding (like a nursing infant).

Anal Stage: This stage occurs during the second and third years of life (so from one to two years of age), the anus is the focus of energy, and the child derives pleasure from the sensation of retaining or expelling feces. The major crisis is toilet training, which is resolved when the child becomes toilet trained.   If toilet training does not go well, the adult leaves too much psychic energy behind at this stage and may develop an anal personality. Specifically, he or she can become anal expulsive (rebellious, messy, prone to temper tantrums and disorganization) or anal retentive (stubborn, stingy, rigid, neat, obstinate, controlling).

Phallic Stage: This stage occurs between the ages of four and six, and the genitals become the focus of energy. The major crisis is the Oedipal complex, which refers to the tendency for the child to become attracted to and desirous of the opposite-sex parent, and jealous of and angry with the same-sex parent. For boys, this crisis is resolved via castration anxiety (the fear that his much more powerful dad will cut off the son's genitals) and the subsequent identification with dad and development of the superego (an internalization of parental standards). For girls, this crisis is resolved when the girl realizes that her dad has a penis (power) and she doesn't, blames her mother (since mom also doesn't have a penis, mom must be to blame), realizes the futility of this, and identifies with her mother (this process is much less clear for girls). The phallic personality who is fixated in this stage is narcissistic, self-centered, vain, and arrogant. He or she needs constant attention and reassurance of his or her attractiveness.

2. There are three major criticisms of psychoanalysis (pp. 478-479). First, it paints a highly pessimistic view of human nature (e.g., we are driven by uncontrollable instincts, our personalities are largely determined by the events of early childhood and thus not capable of much change later in life). Second, psychoanalysis does not meet acceptable standards of science (i.e., it is based largely on after-the-fact theorizing about the early childhoods of mentally disturbed clients). Third, carefully controlled research has largely failed to support most of the basic tenets of Freudian theory. For example, who has ever seen an id? Similarly, parents and children do come into conflict during childhood events, but is it really the result of penis envy or castration anxiety?

Many of Freud's contributions, however, still stand (pp. 479-480). For example, he was one of the first individuals to really demonstrate that mental disorders can have psychological as well as physical origins. He also drew attention to the profound influence that early childhood events can have on personality development. Theoretically, his notion of the mind as an iceberg (levels of consciousness) and his ideas about the power of unconscious forces have continued to inform contemporary work on consciousness, and his work on defense mechanisms also has received support.

194

3. Locus of control refers to people's generalized expectancy for the control of reinforcement (in others words, our beliefs about who is in charge of what happens to us). People with an internal locus of control believe that they themselves are responsible for their outcomes; those with an external locus believe that their outcomes are due to luck, fate, or powerful others (doctors, teachers, officials, parents, etc.). (p. 483)

   Research does suggest that an internal orientation is associated with emotional well-being; control allows us to feel successful, happy, and action-oriented. However, an internal orientation may not always be adaptive. For example, when events are truly uncontrollable, people with an internal orientation have difficulty managing the situation (believing that they are in control, they are incapable of recognizing when they really are not in control, and this may cause them to continue with a maladaptive behavior pattern). Your text mentions that a victim of a crime (a random act that one cannot control) who has an internal orientation (and blames him- or herself) may experience greater distress than someone with an external control (who blames the situation). In addition, having an internal orientation may lead to problems if it causes one to develop an overcontrolling, I'm-always-in-charge kind of style. (pp. 483-484)

4. According to Rogers, we have two competing needs. The first is a natural need for self-actualization, which is the drive to become all that we are capable of becoming and to fulfill our potential. The second is a social drive, conceptualized by Rogers as a need for positive regard (for approval, support, and love) from others. These needs may cause us to experience conflict; for example, if what we want to become or what we actually are is not what others wish us to become or to be (in other words, the positive regard of these others is conditional upon us behaving in a certain way), then we will experience tension and a feeling of discrepancy within the self. (p. 486)

5. Research on twins demonstrates that, for a wide range of traits, identical twins (who share 100 percent of their genetic material) are more similar than fraternal twins (who share less genetic material), and twins raised apart (who are subject to different environmental influences) are as similar as twins raised together (p. 497).

   Research on the personality dimension of introversion-extraversion supports the notion that traits are to some extent biologically influenced. For example, there is growing evidence that introversion-extraversion differences are rooted in differential sensitivities of the central nervous system; introverts possess a CNS that is more sensitive to stimulation (and, indeed, they salivate more than extraverts when exposed to sour tastes, are more easily aroused by stimulant substances, and are less easily relaxed by depressant substances) (pp. 498-500).

CHAPTER 13

PSYCHOLOGICAL DISORDERS

CHAPTER OVERVIEW

This chapter explores the world of psychological disorders, beginning with a discussion of how "normal" and "abnormal" are defined and with an overview of the three major models of abnormality (i.e., medical, psychological, sociocultural). The chapter then considers how to diagnose mental disorders and the impact that diagnostic labels can have on the way that people are perceived and treated. The rest of the chapter is divided among different classes of psychological disorders. First, anxiety disorders (including generalized anxiety disorder, panic disorder, phobic disorder, and obsessive-compulsive disorder) are discussed, followed by somatoform disorders (i.e., hypochondriasis and conversion disorder) and dissociative disorders (amnesia and fugue states, dissociative identity disorder). Next, mood disorders – the prolonged emotional extremes that prevent normal function – are considered. Specifically, your author defines major depression and reviews the biological and psychological explanations for this mood disorder, and discusses its "vicious cycle" and association with suicide. A related mood disorder, bipolar disorder, is also presented. The symptoms, types, and theories of schizophrenia then are discussed, and the chapter ends with a consideration of two personality disorders (borderline, antisocial).

CHAPTER OUTLINE

I. *What's Your Prediction* How Common Are Psychological Disorders?

II. Psychological Disorders: A General Outlook

    A. Defining Normal and Abnormal

    B. Models of Abnormality
        1. The medical perspective
        2. The psychological perspective
        3. The sociocultural perspective
        4. Combining perspectives in a "synthetic" model

    C. Diagnosis: A Necessary Step

III. Anxiety Disorders

    A. Generalized Anxiety Disorder

D. Theories of Schizophrenia
   1. Biological factors
   2. Psychological factors

VIII. Personality Disorders

   A. The Borderline Personality

   B. The Antisocial Personality

   C. *Psychology and Law* The Insanity Defense

IX. Thinking Like a Psychologist About Psychological Disorders

LEARNING OBJECTIVES

By the time you have read and reviewed this chapter, you should be able to:

1. Explain the criteria used by the American Psychiatric Association to determine whether a pattern of behavior can be considered a psychological disorder (pp. 511-512).

2. List and describe the three models of abnormality (i.e., medical, psychological, sociocultural) (pp. 512-514).

3. Explain the basic assumptions of the medical model of abnormality and examine criticisms of this approach (pp. 512-513).

4. Discuss the psychological model of abnormality and consider how psychoanalysis, cognitive social-learning theory, and humanistic psychology understand abnormal behavior (p. 513).

5. Explain the sociocultural perspective and discuss evidence of sociocultural influence on disorders (pp. 513-514).

6. Discuss the "synthesis" model of mental illness (p. 514).

7. Define the term "diagnosis" and discuss the DSM-IV (its uses, contents, and shortcomings) (pp. 514-515). Consider three criticisms of psychiatric diagnoses and labels (pp. 515-516).

8. Distinguish between generalized anxiety disorder, panic disorder, phobic disorder (simple and social), and obsessive-compulsive disorder (pp. 517-522). Consider the causes, symptoms, and treatment of each type of anxiety disorder.

9. Discuss the ways in which anxiety disorders are influenced by the cultural context in which they occur (pp. 523-524).

10. Explain somatoform disorders (pp. 524-525). Distinguish between hypochondriasis (p. 524) and conversion disorder (p. 525) and examine the causes of each type of somatoform disorder.

11. Define dissociative disorders and explain how dissociation may be a "normal" part of daily life (pp. 525-526). Distinguish between amnesia and fugue states (pp. 526-257). Explain the characteristics, possible causes, and diagnostic controversies surrounding dissociative identity disorder (pp. 527-528).

12. List the symptoms of major depressive disorder (p. 529). Identify the correlates of this disorder, including age, gender, and season (pp. 529-530). Examine the biological and psychological causes of major depression (pp. 530-531). Define learned helplessness and the depressive explanatory style (p. 531). Explain the "vicious cycle" of depression and discuss the relation between depression and suicide (pp. 532-533).

13. Consider suicide risk factors and how to respond if you suspect someone you know is suicidal (pp. 534-535).

14. Define bipolar disorder and describe its symptoms. Discuss the genetic basis of this disorder (pp. 533-536).

15. List and describe the five major symptoms of schizophrenic disorders (pp. 538-539). Distinguish between delusions and hallucinations (p. 538). Discuss the five types of schizophrenia and explain the difference between positive and negative symptoms (p. 540). Discuss biological and psychological influences on schizophrenia, and explain the diathesis-stress model (pp. 540-542).

16. Explain the diagnostic criteria for personality disorders (p. 542). List the different types of personality disorders described in the DSM-IV (p. 542).

17. Consider the major features of borderline (p. 543) and antisocial (pp. 543-544) personality disorder. Speculate about the causes of antisocial personality disorder (pp. 545-546).

18. Discuss the concept of insanity and consider the consequences of pleading insanity in a court of law (pp. 544-545). Define the key elements of insanity, from a legal perspective (pp. 544-545). Discuss the problems (e.g., faking) with the insanity defense (p. 545).

19. Discuss how comorbidity can make it difficult to diagnose a disorder (p. 545).

KEY TERMS

The following key terms and concepts are featured in this chapter and are important for you to know. Write out definitions of each term and check your answers with the definitions in the text on the pages listed.

Psychological disorder (p. 511)
Medical model (p. 512)
Psychological model (p. 512)
Sociocultural model (p. 512)
Culture-bound syndromes (p. 514)
Diagnosis (p. 514)
DSM-IV (p. 514)
Generalized anxiety disorder (p. 517)
Panic disorder (p. 519)
Agoraphobia (p. 519)
Phobic disorder (p. 519)
Simple phobia (p. 519)
Social phobia (p. 519)
Obsessive-compulsive disorder (OCD) (p. 521)
Somatoform disorder (p. 524)
Hypochondriasis (p. 524)
Conversion disorder (p. 525)
Dissociative disorder (p. 526)
Amnesia (p. 526)
Fugue state (p. 526)
Dissociative identity disorder (DID) (p. 527)
Mood disorder (p. 529)
Depression (p. 529)
Learned helplessness (p. 531)
Depressive explanatory style (p. 531)
Bipolar disorder (p. 532)
Schizophrenic disorders (p. 536)
Delusions (p. 538)
Hallucinations (p. 538)
Diathesis-stress model (p. 541)
Personality disorder (p. 542)
Borderline personality disorder (p. 542)
Antisocial personality disorder (p. 542)
Comorbidity (p. 546)

TEST QUESTIONS

Multiple-Choice Questions

Circle the correct choice for each question and compare your answers with those at the end of the Study Guide chapter.

1. Women are more likely than men to experience _____; men are more likely than women to experience _____.
   a. anxiety; depression
   b. antisocial personality disorder; substance abuse
   c. depression; substance abuse
   d. schizophrenia; anxiety

2. According to the APA, a pattern of behavior that _____ may be classified as a psychological disorder.
   a. results in an increased risk of death
   b. is not a "normal" response to specific life events
   c. is not a deliberate reaction to social conditions
   d. All of the above

3. A doctor who views anxiety as the result of a neurotransmitter imbalance and who treats this disorder with drugs is following the _____ model.
   a. medical
   b. psychological
   c. sociocultural
   d. demonology

4. A doctor who views anxiety as a learned response to situations is following the _____ model of abnormality.
   a. medical
   b. psychological
   c. sociocultural
   d. demonology

5. Which of the following provides evidence that supports the sociocultural model of abnormality?
   a. Anxiety is found in all cultures around the world.
   b. Emotional problems occur in teenagers from all racial, ethnic, and cultural groups.
   c. Anorexia is almost exclusively found in Western cultures.
   d. All of the above

6. A major criticism of early versions of the DSM was that they
   a. could only be used to make diagnoses of individuals from Western cultures.
   b. were based on anecdotal evidence.
   c. had low levels of reliability.
   d. could only be used to make diagnoses of male patients.

7. Your text describes a study conducted by Rosenhan (1973) in which he and his colleagues were admitted to mental hospitals after complaining of certain symptoms. What was the main point of this classic study?
   a. Once a diagnostic label is applied to someone ("schizophrenic"), all behavior comes to be seen in terms of that label.
   b. It is hard to tell the difference between "normal" and "abnormal" behavior.
   c. The DSM cannot be used reliably to diagnose schizophrenia.
   d. Most people in psychiatric hospitals are not mentally ill.

8. Izzy has just finished reading the chapter in her psychology textbook on psychological disorders and now she is convinced that she is suffering from several mental disorders. It is likely that she is experiencing _____.
   a. generalized anxiety disorder
   b. major depression
   c. hyperactivity
   d. medical student's disease

9. Kess goes through each day feeling uneasy and tense. She is very sensitive to criticism and has difficulty making decisions, even about little things. She constantly worries about her job, her financial situation, and family matters. Her symptoms fit the diagnostic category of
   a. generalized anxiety disorder.
   b. major depression.
   c. phobic disorder.
   d. somatoform disorder.

10. Which item is out of place here?
    a. phobic disorder
    b. panic disorder
    c. seasonal affective disorder
    d. obsessive-compulsive disorder

11. One day during his lunch hour, Robert suddenly couldn't breathe. He felt his heart racing, he began to hyperventilate, and he became worried that he was dying. He wanted to get help from his coworkers, but he was worried about embarrassing himself in front of them. If these episodes continue, Robert might be diagnosed with _____.
    a. bipolar disorder
    b. panic disorder
    c. generalized anxiety disorder
    d. simple phobia

12. Patricia seldom leaves her home. She works out of a home office, has friends visit her at home, and has most things delivered to her. The idea of being in a movie theater, going to a public park, or eating in a restaurant, scares her. Such symptoms are typical of
    a. obsessive-compulsive disorder.
    b. agoraphobia.
    c. fugue states.
    d. panic disorder.

13. All during the day, Don has repetitive thoughts about dirt and germs. To deal with these unpleasant images, he carefully washes and disinfects his hands precisely three times each hour. Don's thoughts reflect _____ and his washing behavior reflects _____.
    a. generalized anxiety; panic disorder
    b. an obsession; a compulsion
    c. a simple phobia; a social phobia
    d. a compulsion; an obsession

14. Chuck complains of numbness and tingling in his fingertips, nausea, chest pains, and indigestion. He is intensely aware of his own bodily sensations, often becoming extremely alarmed the moment that he sneezes or coughs. Certain that he suffers from extremely poor health, Chuck has seen over a dozen doctors in the past two years. Chuck may have
    a. hypochondriasis.
    b. a social phobia.
    c. paranoid schizophrenia.
    d. bipolar disorder.

15. Jana's son was recently bitten by a snake. Although she tried to hit the snake with her fist before it reached her child, Jana was unable to prevent it from biting him. Her son is fine, but Jana's hand has become paralyzed. However, examination and testing show no physical damage to her hand. Jana's paralysis may reflect
    a. psychosomatic disorder.
    b. hypochondriasis.
    c. insanity.
    d. conversion disorder.

16. While driving to work one day, Eli debates what color to paint his new house. When he arrives at his parking spot, he realizes that he doesn't remember any of the details of his drive in to work. Eli has experienced
    a. a manic episode.
    b. an obsessive thought.
    c. dissociation.
    d. a fugue state.

17. During a soccer game at the local park, Sheila is hit on the head by the ball. For a short time afterward, she cannot remember the name of the park, nor the name and mascot of her soccer team. However, she remembers who she is and where she lives. Later, her memory clears up. This condition is called
    a. a fugue state.
    b. amnesia.
    c. dissociative identity disorder.
    d. dissociative amnesia.

18. After several years of living and working in a small town in Michigan, Paul wakes up one morning insisting that his name is Brian and that he has to report to his job in Atlanta, Georgia. He does not recognize the furniture in his apartment or the clothing hanging in his closet. He is completely confused about his current life. He may have experienced
    a. a fugue state.
    b. dissociative identity disorder.
    c. borderline personality.
    d. amnesia.

19. Which statement best describes dissociative identity disorder?
    a. The individual loses contact with reality and becomes incapable of perceiving objective events.
    b. The person often moves to a new community and takes on a new identity for a period of time.
    c. The individual seems to have two or more distinct psychological selves or identities.
    d. The individual's personality "splits" into two halves, one that is emotional and one that is cognitive.

20. Many clinicians and researchers are skeptical about the recent increase in diagnoses of dissociative identity disorder (DID) because
    a. examples of people with this condition cannot be found earlier than 1970.
    b. some patients have faked multiple personalities for personal gain.
    c. people with DID are often hypochondriacs.
    d. this condition exists only in Western cultures.

21. Glynnis just doesn't enjoy doing much of anything lately. She blames herself for all her failures in life. She has lost interest in food and social activities, and most days she just stays in bed. If these symptoms last for more than two weeks, she may be diagnosed as having
    a. bipolar disorder.
    b. antisocial personality.
    c. major depression.
    d. agoraphobia.

22. If one identical twin is diagnosed with depression, the likelihood that the other twin also will develop this disorder is
    a. 10 percent.
    b. 50 percent.
    c. 75 percent.
    d. 100 percent.

23. The phrase "vicious cycle of depression" refers to the fact that depressed people
    a. dislike social support and refuse to interact with their friends and partners.
    b. have learned to become helpless in the face of adversity.
    c. are prone to become aggressive and vicious toward others.
    d. need social support but behave in ways that almost always result in social rejection.

24. Which one of the following statements about suicide is inaccurate?
    a. More men than women complete their attempted suicides.
    b. More women than men attempt suicide.
    c. Depression is not associated with suicide attempts.
    d. One of the best predictors of suicide is a sense of hopelessness.

25. Mardie hasn't slept in several days. She alternates between writing what she believes will be a grammy-winning album of folk songs and going on expensive shopping sprees. She speaks in a loud, frenzied voice and explodes in anger when her roommate tells her to "calm down." If this pattern is followed by a period of depression, a diagnosis of _____ may be made.
    a. bipolar disorder
    b. major depression
    c. dissociative identity disorder
    d. seasonal affective disorder

26. The "split" in schizophrenia involves a split
    a. between two or more inner selves.
    b. between the two hemispheres of the cerebral cortex.
    c. between one's masculine and feminine traits and characteristics.
    d. between the various brain functions.

27. Which of the following symptoms often are observed in people with a schizophrenic disorder?
    a. incoherent thinking and bizarre behavior
    b. delusions and hallucinations
    c. disturbed affect
    d. All of the above

28. While completing your internship at a state institution, you observe a young man complaining about how the other patients are spying on him and trying to poison him. He is highly suspicious of other people and he also believes that the government is monitoring his activities through the television set. These features are characteristic of _____ schizophrenia.
    a. catatonic
    b. paranoid
    c. disorganized
    d. undifferentiated

29. When a person's overall behavior patterns are inflexible and maladaptive and cause distress, the person may be diagnosed with
    a. schizophrenia.
    b. dissociative identity disorder.
    c. a personality disorder.
    d. fugues.

30. Michelle has difficulty maintaining friendships and romantic relationships. She is uncertain about her own identity and about her goals in life, experiences extreme mood fluctuations, and is prone to inappropriate outbursts of anger. When Michelle meets a potential new friend, partner, or colleague, she clings to that person so fiercely that he or she becomes alienated and leaves the relationship. Michelle may have
    a. borderline personality disorder.
    b. antisocial personality disorder.
    c. disorganized schizophrenia.
    d. mania.

True-False Questions

Indicate which of the following statements are true or false, and compare your answers with those at the end of the chapter.

T F   1. Men and women are equally likely to develop a psychological disorder over the course of their lifetimes.

T F   2. There is a clear and distinct division between "normal" and "abnormal" behavior.

T F 3. There are a number of psychological models of abnormality.

T F 4. Clinical judgments may be biased by expectations, stereotypes, and diagnostic labels.

T F 5. Research suggests that phobias can be learned through classical conditioning and observation.

T F 6. The physiological symptoms of anxiety vary across cultures.

T F 7. There is some evidence that hypochondriasis is associated with nervous system oversensitivity.

T F 8. Dissociative identity disorder is one of the most common psychological disorders.

T F 9. Depression appears to be linked to both biological and psychological factors.

T F 10. People diagnosed with one disorder often have symptoms of others as well.

Key Concepts Matching Exercises

Exercise #1: Diagnosis

Match the psychological disorders listed on the left with the definitions or examples listed on the right.

_____ 1. Generalized anxiety disorder   a. "I don't know who I am or what I want to be. I'm moody, and I can't seem to maintain a relationship even though I desperately want one."

_____ 2. Panic disorder   b. "I'm glad summer is here. I always feel better in the summer. Winter gets me down."

_____ 3. Agoraphobia   c. "How am I? Just terrible! I'm sure I'm coming down with something – I've had this tight feeling in my throat all day and my skin is tingly. I think I have that new virus that's been in the news lately."

_____ 4. Obsessive-compulsive disorder   d. "Oh my gosh, am I having a heart attack? I can't breathe, I can't think, my throat is closing up. I think I'm going to pass out!"

_____ 5. Hypochondriasis   e. "Why are you calling me 'Betty'? My name is Veronica. Whose clothes are these? They aren't mine – and I don't live in California, I'm from Massachusetts."

_____ 6. Conversion disorder

_____ 7. Amnesia

_____ 8. Fugue state

_____ 9. Dissociative identity disorder

_____ 10. Depression

_____ 11. Bipolar disorder

_____ 12. Seasonal affective disorder

_____ 13. Paranoid schizophrenia

_____ 14. Residual schizophrenia

_____ 15. Borderline personality

_____ 16. Antisocial personality

f. "One day I'm on top of the world, and the next I'm plunged into the depths of despair."

g. "Ever since I saw that terrible car accident, I've been blind."

h. "Well, I had some schizophrenic symptoms a few years ago, but the drugs seem to be working. I haven't had any major symptoms since then."

i. "Did I turn off the oven last night? I'd better check." "Maybe the oven is still on. I'd better check one more time."

j. "Sonny isn't here right now. I'm here, and my name is Justin. When I leave, you can talk with Sonny again."

k. "Did I hit my head? I can't remember any of the details."

l. "I am so worried about everything – my car, my life, my job, my relationships, my pets, my own health. Everything seems to be a source of constant anxiety."

m. "I don't care about you. You exist only to serve my needs. I feel no guilt or remorse whatsoever. People get what they deserve, and I deserve everything."

n. "I can't seem to get up enough energy to do anything. My whole life is one big failure. Just leave me alone."

o. "Are you following me? Stop talking about me behind my back! I know I'm being watched. I hear the voices, and I see the signs."

p. "Oh no, I could never go out in public. The mere thought of being surrounded by all those people makes me really uncomfortable. I'd much rather stay at home, where it's safe."

Essay Questions

Write out answers to the following brief essay questions. Compare your responses with the sample answers at the end of the Study Guide chapter.

1. When is a pattern of behavior considered to be a psychological disorder, according to the American Psychiatric Association? Is there always a clear distinction between "normal" and "abnormal" behavior? Explain, using a specific example, how the same behavior could be viewed as "normal" in one situation and "abnormal" in another.

2. What are the three major concerns that critics have voiced about psychiatric diagnosis in general and about using the DSM in particular?

3. In what way is anxiety a universal phenomenon? In what way is it culture-specific?

4. Explain the "vicious cycle" of depression.

5. Consider the biological basis of schizophrenia. What is the diathesis-stress model?

TEST SOLUTIONS

Multiple-Choice Solutions

1. c (p. 510)	11. b (p. 518)	21. c (p. 529)
2. d (pp. 511-512)	12. b (p. 519)	22. b (p. 530)
3. a (pp. 512-513)	13. b (p. 521)	23. d (p. 532)
4. b (p. 513)	14. a (p. 524)	24. c (p. 532)
5. c (pp. 513-514)	15. d (p. 525)	25. a (pp. 533-535)
6. c (pp. 515-516)	16. c (pp. 525-526)	26. d (p. 537)
7. a (p. 516)	17. b (p. 526)	27. d (p. 538)
8. d (p. 517)	18. a (p. 526)	28. b (p. 540)
9. a (p. 517)	19. c (p. 527)	29. c (p. 542)
10. c (pp. 518-521)	20. b (p. 527)	30. a (p. 543)

True-False Solutions

1. T (p. 510)	6. F (p. 523)
2. F (pp. 512, 546)	7. T (pp. 524-525)
3. T (p. 512)	8. F (p. 526)
4. T (p. 516)	9. T (pp. 530-531)
5. T (p. 520)	10. T (p. 546)

Key Concepts Matching Solutions

Exercise #1

1. l	9. j
2. d	10. n
3. p	11. f
4. i	12. b
5. c	13. o
6. g	14. h
7. k	15. a
8. e	16. m

Essay Solutions

1. According to the American Psychiatric Association, a pattern of behavior can be considered a psychological disorder if it satisfies three conditions. First, the person must experience significant pain or distress, an inability to work or play, an increased risk of death, or a loss of freedom in important areas in life. Second, the source of the problem must reside within the person (as the result of biological factors, learned habits, or mental processes) and must not be a reaction to specific life events (like the loss of a loved one). Third, the behavior must not be a deliberate reaction to conditions like poverty, prejudice, government policy, or other conflicts with society. (pp. 511-512)

   There really is no clear dividing line between "normal" and "abnormal" behavior; that is, although it is possible to identify behavior that is clearly abnormal, these labels lie upon a continuum. Thus, it is difficult, for example, to determine how much anxiety is "normal" and how much is "abnormal." (p. 512)

   You should select an example of a behavior that can be viewed as normal in one situation and as a disorder in another. In thinking of relatively recent events in the media, one example might be cannibalistic behavior (eating human flesh). Serial killer Jeffrey Dahmer (who was convicted of murder) engaged in cannibalistic behavior – he ate pieces of his victims' bodies. This behavior was clearly abnormal – the source of the behavior resided within him, and it was not a reaction to a specific life event (like poverty, starvation, etc.). The cannibalistic behavior of the surviving members of a soccer team whose plane crashed in the Andes (featured in the movie "Alive") is unpleasant to think about, but is not due to a psychological disorder. The behavior in this case came about as a result of a specific life event (the plane crash), was a deliberate reaction to a social condition (starvation, potential death), and did not continue once that condition was removed (the individuals were rescued).

2. The first major concern is that the diagnostic system, which is based on the DSM-IV, lacks reliability. Research on the first editions of the DSM demonstrated that the instrument lacked high reliability; however, later editions appear to produce higher reliability. The second concern involves the issue of bias. Research provides strong evidence that clinical judgments and diagnoses are influenced by stereotypes, expectations, and all the other biases that affect human judgment and decision making (after all, clinicians are human, too, and subject to the same factors that affect the rest of us). For example, some studies find that the same symptoms are labeled "antisocial personality" (which is more common among men than women) when the patient is male and "histrionic personality" (which is more common among women than men) when the patient is female. The third concern is related to the second, and involves the notion that diagnostic labels can adversely affect the way that we perceive and treat those with a particular disorder; in other words, we might view the most innocuous behaviors as "evidence" that someone is depressed, for example, if we have already been told that the person is depressed. (pp. 515-516)

3. Anxiety is a universal phenomenon in two ways. First, anxiety is experienced by all people, of all ages, around the world (p. 523). Second, the physiological symptoms of anxiety (e.g., shortness of breath, racing heart, trembling) are the same across cultures (p. 523). However, anxiety is also a culture-specific phenomenon in terms of its cognitive component – as noted by your textbook author, the types of symptoms that cause people anxiety, the interpretations placed on those symptoms, and beliefs about the causes of anxiety are different in different cultures. For example, *Koro* (the anxiety-producing belief that one's sexual organs will disappear into the body and cause death) is specific to Asian cultures, *susto* (an intense fear reaction brought on by the belief that one has been cursed by voodoo or black magic) is found in Central and Latin American cultures, and so on (p. 523).

4. The "vicious cycle" of depression refers to the fact that many men and women with depression are in desperate need of social support and friendship, but they behave in ways that almost always prevent them from achieving these things. In other words, depression causes social rejection, which increases the depression, which in turn causes more social rejection, and so on. There is research that people who are depressed avoid eye contact, speak softly, are slow to respond to others, and are negative in their emotional expressions and demeanor. They also tend to withdraw socially (one of the major symptoms of depression). All of these factors prevent successful social contact. Others may interpret these behaviors as a sign of rudeness, detachment, and a desire to be left alone (when in fact the opposite is often the case). The result is that people may react to depressed others with mixed emotions – sadness, a desire to help, irritation, anger, etc. (p. 532)

5. Schizophrenia has a strong genetic basis (the more closely related you are to someone with schizophrenia, the higher the likelihood that you will develop schizophrenia yourself). In addition, there are clear biological factors involved in this disorder, most notably an excess of, or an oversensitivity to, the neurotransmitter dopamine and structural defects in the brain (pp. 540-541). However, there is also evidence for the impact of environmental or psychological factors in the development of schizophrenia (just because one identical twin has schizophrenia does not necessarily mean the other twin will develop it). The diathesis-stress model states that schizophrenia is the result of both a genetic, biological, or acquired predisposition (diathesis) toward schizophrenia and an environmental stressor (stress) that causes that predisposition to actually develop (p. 541).

CHAPTER 14

TREATMENT

CHAPTER OVERVIEW

In the last chapter, you were introduced to a variety of psychological disorders – their symptoms, prevalence, and causes. This chapter explores the many therapeutic approaches that have been developed to treat these disorders. The majority of the chapter is devoted to psychotherapy, or those forms of treatment that utilize psychological techniques. Your author discusses the major techniques and assumptions of both orthodox (classic Freudian) and modified (brief) psychoanalytic therapies, considers the criticisms and legacies of these forms of psychotherapy, and reviews research on the phenomenon of repressed memory. Next, the chapter explores behavioral therapies, including classical-conditioning techniques (i.e., flooding, systematic desensitization, aversive conditioning) and operant-conditioning methods (i.e., reinforcement programs or token economies, punishment, biofeedback techniques, social-skills training). Cognitive therapies, which focus on altering maladaptive thought patterns, then are presented. Specifically, your author discusses Ellis's rational-emotive behavior therapy and Beck's cognitive therapy. The last psychotherapeutic approach to be discussed is the humanistic perspective. The assumptions and techniques of person-centered therapy (associated with Rogers) and Gestalt therapy (associated with Perls) are presented. Then, the chapter explores a variety of group therapy approaches, including self-help groups and family therapy. At this point, your author considers the effectiveness of psychotherapy in general, whether one type of therapy is better than another, and the essential ingredients of a successful therapy. This section ends with a discussion of current trends in psychotherapy; namely, eclecticism. The final part of the chapter focuses on medical interventions, including drug therapies, electroconvulsive therapy, and psychosurgery.

CHAPTER OUTLINE

I. *What's Your Prediction Consumer Reports* Asks, Does Psychotherapy Help?

II. Psychological Therapies

      A. Psychoanalytic Therapies
            1. Orthodox psychoanalysis
                 a. Free association
                 b. Resistance
                 c. Transference
            2. Brief psychoanalytic therapies
            3. Controversies in psychoanalysis

B. Behavioral Therapies
    1. Classical-conditioning techniques
        a. Flooding
        b. Systematic desensitization
        c. Aversive conditioning
    2. Operant-conditioning techniques
        a. Reward and punishment
        b. Biofeedback
        c. Social-skills training

C. *Psychology and Law* Putting Repressed Memories on Trial

D. *How To* Use Biofeedback to Treat Headaches

E. Cognitive Therapies
    1. Rational-emotive behavior therapy
    2. Beck's cognitive therapy

F. *The Process of Discovery* Aaron T. Beck

G. Humanistic Therapies
    1. Person-centered therapy
    2. Gestalt therapy

H. Group-Therapy Approaches

III. Perspectives on Psychotherapy

A. The Bottom Line: Does Psychotherapy Work?

B. Are Some Therapies Better than Others?

C. What Are the Active Ingredients?
    1. A supportive relationship
    2. A ray of hope
    3. An opportunity to open up

D. What's the Future of Psychotherapy?

IV. Medical Interventions

A. Drug Therapies
    1. Antianxiety drugs
    2. Antidepressants

3. Mood stabilizers
4. Antipsychotic drugs

B. *How To* Beat the Winter Blues

C. Perspectives on Drug Therapies

D. Electroconvulsive Therapy

E. Psychosurgery

V. Thinking Like a Psychologist About Treatment

LEARNING OBJECTIVES

By the time you have read and reviewed this chapter, you should be able to:

1. Consider the various methods that historically were used to treat mental illness (pp. 553-554) and discuss two developments that led to the creation of the two dominant modern methods for treating psychological disorders (pp. 553-554).

2. Define the term psychotherapy and list the various types of professionals who can conduct psychotherapy (p. 554).

3. Describe the goals of orthodox (classical Freudian) psychoanalysis (p. 555). List and describe the three types of behavior – free association, resistance, transference – that a traditional psychoanalyst interprets during therapy (pp. 555-556).

4. Compare orthodox and brief psychoanalytic therapies (pp. 557-558).

5. Consider the three main criticisms of psychoanalysis as a form of treatment (p. 558). Consider the impact that psychoanalysis has had on clinical theories, practice, and research (p. 558).

6. Describe the basic assumptions of the behavioral therapies, and compare them with the assumptions of psychoanalysis (pp. 558-559).

7. List and describe the three classical-conditioning therapies (pp. 559, 562-564).

8. Describe the technique of flooding (p. 559).

9. Describe the phenomenon of repressed memory and consider the controversy surrounding repressed memories. List the conclusions about the issue drawn by the APA taskforce (pp. 560-561).

10. Consider the three steps involved in systematic desensitization (i.e., relaxation training, anxiety hierarchy creation, gradual exposure) (p. 562).

11. Explain the technique of aversive conditioning (p. 564).

12. Describe operant-conditioning techniques, including the ways in which reinforcement (token economies), punishment, biofeedback, and social-skills training can be used to change abnormal behavior (pp. 564-565).

13. Consider how biofeedback may be used to treat migraine headaches (p. 566).

14. Discuss the basic tenet of cognitive therapies (p. 567).

15. Describe rational-emotive behavior therapy (REBT) and compare this technique with Beck's cognitive therapy (pp. 567-569). Consider other forms of cognitive therapy (e.g., stress-inoculation training) (p. 569).

16. List and describe the four assumptions and goals of humanistic therapy (p. 571).

17. Describe the features of person-centered therapy, including empathy, unconditional positive regard, genuineness, and reflection (p. 571).

18. Explain the features of Gestalt therapy and compare this approach with that of person-centered therapy (pp. 571-573).

19. Consider the features of family therapies (pp. 574-575).

20. Consider the question of whether psychotherapy "works" (pp. 575-576). Explain why researchers are cautious about using clients' self-reports as a measure of the effectiveness of psychotherapy (pp. 575-576).

21. Discuss whether some therapies might be more effective than others (pp. 576-577).

22. Explain the three features common to all successful psychotherapies (pp. 577-578).

23. Describe the eclectic approach to psychotherapy (pp. 578-579).

24. Identify the three types of medical interventions used to treat abnormal behavior (p. 580).

25. Distinguish among the various types of drug therapies, including those used to treat anxiety, to treat depression, to stabilize mood, and to reduce the positive symptoms of schizophrenia (pp. 580-584).

26. Consider whether drug therapy or psychotherapy is the preferable form of treatment for psychological disorders (p. 585).

27. Describe electroconvulsive therapy – its history, procedures, and uses (pp. 585-586).

28. Define psychosurgery and explain why this is a controversial form of medical intervention. Consider its uses (p. 586).

29. Consider the various treatment options now available to consumers (p. 587).

KEY TERMS

The following key terms and concepts are featured in this chapter and are important for you to know. Write out definitions of each term and check your answers with the definitions in the text on the pages listed.

Psychotherapy (p. 554)
Free association (p. 554)
Resistance (p. 556)
Transference (p. 556)
Behavioral therapy or cognitive-behavioral therapy (p. 559)
Flooding (p. 559)
Systematic desensitization (p. 559)
Aversion therapy (p. 564)
Token economy (p. 564)
Biofeedback (p. 565)
Social-skills training (p. 565)
Cognitive therapy (p. 567)
Rational-emotive behavior therapy (REBT) (p. 567)
Person-centered therapy (p. 571)
Gestalt therapy (p. 571)
Group therapy (p. 573)
Family therapies (p. 574)
Placebo effect (p. 578)
Psychopharmacology (p. 580)
Antianxiety drugs (p. 581)
Antidepressants (p. 581)
Seasonal affective disorder (SAD) (p. 582)
Lithium (p. 582)
Antipsychotic drugs (p. 583)
Electroconvulsive therapy (ECT) (p. 585)
Psychosurgery (p. 586)

TEST QUESTIONS

Multiple-Choice Questions
Circle the correct choice for each question and compare your answers with those at the end of the Study Guide chapter.

1. The goal of psychoanalytic therapy is
    a. insight.
    b. catharsis.
    c. free association.
    d. a and b

2. In order to deal with his recurrent bouts of anxiety, Charley is seeing a psychoanalyst. During each session, Dr. Farley encourages Charley to lie back, relax, and say whatever comes to his mind. This part of psychoanalysis is called _____.
    a. resistance
    b. free association
    c. transference
    d. catharsis

3. After about six months of therapy, Charley finds himself becoming more and more upset with Dr. Farley. Dr. Farley believes that Charley is really angry with his father and that the feelings he has for his therapist reflect _____.
    a. resistance
    b. insight
    c. transference
    d. catharsis

4. When Dr. Farley suggests that Charley may have some buried feelings of anger and hostility toward his father, Charley laughs and quickly changes the subject. This happens several times. Charley's behavior may reflect
    a. transference.
    b. resistance.
    c. insight.
    d. catharsis.

5. Compared to traditional Freudian techniques, modern psychoanalytic therapies
    a. are less time-consuming and intense.
    b. focus more heavily on current life problems.
    c. minimize the use of transference and resistance.
    d. All of the above

6. A task force assembled by the APA reviewed evidence on repressed memories of childhood abuse. What conclusions did they draw?
    a. Most people who were abused as children remember all or part of what happened.
    b. It is possible to recall old memories that have been forgotten over time.
    c. It is possible to construct false memories of events that did not occur.
    d. All of the above

7. Which of the following is out of place?
    a. flooding
    b. token economies
    c. systematic desensitization
    d. aversive conditioning

8. Sharon is extremely afraid of snakes. To eliminate her phobia, the therapist locks her in a room with a caged snake. Although she experiences an initial panic reaction, her fear subsides after 45 minutes. This procedure is repeated several times until the phobia is completely gone. The therapist has used the classical conditioning technique of

    _____.
    a. flooding
    b. systematic desensitization
    c. anxiety hierarchies
    d. relaxation training

9. Lee is also extremely afraid of snakes and has sought treatment for his phobia. During his therapy, he is trained in relaxation techniques, he and his therapist construct an anxiety hierarchy, and he is gradually exposed over several sessions to the items on the anxiety hierarchy. Lee has experienced _____.
    a. flooding
    b. aversion therapy
    c. systematic desensitization
    d. modeling

10. Nick signs up for a program that promises to help him quit smoking. At his first treatment session he is placed in a small room and told to start smoking his cigarettes and to keep smoking them until the doctor tells him to stop. The room quickly fills with smoke and after a short time Nick starts to feel sick. This occurs for several more treatment sessions. Nick has experienced _____.
    a. flooding
    b. aversion therapy
    c. systematic desensitization
    d. modeling

11. Donna works with autistic children. When a child engages in "good" behavior (for example, picking up his or her toys), she gives the child a plastic chip that can be exchanged for television privileges, candy, and other treats. Donna has established a _____.
    a. biofeedback system
    b. token economy
    c. social skills workshop
    d. conditioning system

12. Ryan was diagnosed with schizophrenia a few years ago. In order to help Ryan learn how to more effectively interact with people, his therapist demonstrates appropriate forms of eye contact, social distance, and conversational style. Ryan then imitates and rehearses the same behaviors while his therapist provides praise and constructive feedback. Ryan is receiving _____.
    a. social-skills training
    b. biofeedback
    c. interpersonal perception training
    d. systematic sensitization

13. Which one of the following statements about cognitive therapy is accurate?
    a. Cognitive therapy is long-term therapy.
    b. Cognitive therapy centers on unconscious conflicts rooted in early childhood.
    c. Cognitive therapy is designed to alter maladaptive thought processes and beliefs.
    d. Cognitive therapy focuses on concrete behaviors that can be changed via conditioning principles.

14. Jay is about to begin rational-emotive behavior therapy. Which of the following might he expect to experience during the course of his treatment?
    a. flooding
    .b. pain exercises
    c. psychoeducation
    d. catharsis

15. Compared with Ellis's rational-emotive therapy, Beck's cognitive therapy is
    a. less successful.
    b. gentler and more collaborative.
    c. more behaviorally-oriented.
    d. less focused on changing cognitions.

16. Rogers redefined the role of the therapist as being that of a(n) _____.
    a. detective
    b. adviser
    c. teacher
    d. facilitator

220

17. Person-centered therapists must demonstrate which quality for a successful therapeutic experience?
    a. unconditional positive regard
    b. genuineness
    c. empathy
    d. All of the above

18. The technique of _____ involves actively listening to a client's statements without interrupting or evaluating, paraphrasing those statements in response to the client, and seeking clarification when needed.
    a. reflection
    b. transference
    c. unconditional regard
    d. empathic interaction

19. Which of the following individuals would play the least directive role in the therapeutic process?
    a. Lisa, a Beckian cognitive therapist
    b. Louie, a rational-emotive therapist
    c. Lana, a person-centered therapist
    d. Luke, a psychoanalyst

20. Compared to Rogerian therapy, Gestalt therapy is
    a. more confrontational.
    b. less directive.
    c. more focused on early childhood experience.
    d. All of the above

21. Alcoholics Anonymous is a(n)
    a. encounter group.
    b. self-help group.
    c. person-centered group.
    d. family group.

22. Family therapies view the family as
    a. a "salad" composed of individual, separate ingredients.
    b. a "universe" composed of distinct planets.
    c. a "system" composed of interdependent parts.
    d. a "battleground" composed of warring factions.

23. Research by Eysenck showed that people who were on waiting lists for therapy, but had not yet been actually treated, were
    a. more likely to have shown improvement than those who had started therapy.
    b. less likely to have shown improvement than those who had started therapy.
    c. just as likely to have shown improvement as those who had started therapy.
    d. none of the above

24. Cognitive therapies appear to be most effective for treating
    a. phobic disorders.
    b. depression.
    c. low self-esteem.
    d. obsessive-compulsive disorder.

25. Behavioral therapies are most effective at treating
    a. mood disorders.
    b. anxiety disorders.
    c. low self-esteem.
    d. repressed hostility.

26. Which term is out of place?
    a. drug therapy
    b. ECT
    c. REBT
    d. psychosurgery

27. Generalized anxiety disorder is to benzodiazepines as bipolar disorder is to _____.
    a. lithium
    b. barbiturates
    c. prozac
    d. thorazine

28. Parker is taking chlorpromazine for schizophrenia. What might he expect to experience?
    a. reduced negative symptoms
    b. increased negative symptoms
    c. reduced muscle control
    d. increased positive symptoms

29. A consideration in using drug therapy is
    a. side effects.
    b. physical dependence.
    c. psychological dependence.
    d. All of the above

30. Electroconvulsive therapy (ECT) is likely to result in which of the following?
   a. a temporary state of confusion
   b. death
   c. severe brain damage
   d. significant alterations in personality

True-False Questions

Indicate which of the following statements are true or false, and compare your answers with those at the end of the chapter.

T F 1. Survey reports indicate that most people are satisfied with the outcomes of their therapy.

T F 2. Modern psychoanalysis has eliminated the classic Freudian focus on unconscious processes and past experiences.

T F 3. Psychoanalysis is on the increase in the United States.

T F 4. It is possible to create a memory for an event that did not take place.

T F 5. Systematic desensitization is a highly effective form of treatment for phobias.

T F 6. Biofeedback allows people to control parts of the autonomic nervous system.

T F 7. Cognitive therapy is the most frequently taught orientation in American clinical psychology graduate programs.

T F 8. Research suggests that no single therapeutic approach is consistently superior to another.

T F 9. Most psychotherapists identify themselves with a single orientation (e.g., cognitive, behavioral, Freudian).

T F 10. The number of people who seek professional help for psychological problems has increased in recent years.

Key Concepts Matching Exercises

Exercise #1: Psychotherapy

Match the disorders or phenomena listed on the right with the most effective treatment. Each treatment may be used for more than one disorder.

_____ 1. Psychoanalysis   a. obsessive-compulsive disorder

_____ 2. Behavioral therapies   b. repressed conflicts

_____ 3. Cognitive therapies   c. low self-esteem

_____ 4. Humanistic therapies   d. depression

                                    e. unconscious anxiety

                                    f. phobias

Exercise #2: Drug Therapies

Match the drug therapy listed on the left with the symptoms it relieves, disorders it treats, and effects it produces.

_____ 1. Benzodiazepines   a. mood stabilizer

_____ 2. Prozac   b. tranquilizing agent

_____ 3. Lithium   c. used to treat schizophrenia

_____ 4. Thorazine   d. reduces manic symptoms

                                    e. produces mood elevation

                                    f. used to treat bipolar disorder

                                    g. reduces hallucinations and delusions

                                    h. used to treat generalized anxiety disorder

                                    i. may relieve depression

Essay Questions

Write out answers to the following brief essay questions. Compare your responses with the sample answers at the end of the Study Guide chapter.

1. Discuss how modern psychoanalysis differs from traditional Freudian psychoanalysis. In what ways does modern psychoanalysis resemble traditional psychoanalysis?

2. Toby is terribly afraid of spiders. In fact, his fear is so excessive that he decided to take a leave of absence from his job at the local zoo when he learned that a new exhibit on spiders would soon open. Desperately seeking a cure for his phobia, he turns to you for help. Explain how you would use systematic desensitization to treat Toby.

3. What is a token economy? Is it ever appropriate to use punishment as a form of therapy?

4. What four features characterize the humanistic approach to therapy? How is person-centered therapy different from Gestalt therapy?

5. Consider the positive and negative aspects of drug therapies.

TEST SOLUTIONS

Multiple-Choice Solutions

1. d (p. 555)	11. b (p. 564)	21. b (p. 574)
2. b (p. 555)	12. a (p. 565)	22. c (p. 574)
3. c (p. 556)	13. c (p. 567)	23. c (p. 576)
4. b (p. 556)	14. c (p. 568)	24. b (p. 577)
5. d (pp. 557-558)	15. b (p. 568)	25. b (p. 577)
6. d (p. 561)	16. d (p. 571)	26. c (p. 580)
7. b (pp. 559, 562-564)	17. d (p. 571)	27. a (pp. 581-582)
8. a (p. 559)	18. a (p. 571)	28. c (p. 584)
9. c (p. 562)	19. c (p. 571)	29. d (pp. 584-585)
10. b (p. 564)	20. a (p. 571)	30. a (p. 586)

True-False Solutions

1. T (p. 552)	6. T (p. 566)
2. F (p. 558)	7. T (p. 569)
3. F (p. 558)	8. T (p. 577)
4. T (p. 561)	9. F (p. 579)
5. T (p. 563)	10. T (p. 587)

Key Concepts Matching Solutions

Exercise #1	Exercise #2
1. b, e	1. b, h
2. a, f	2. e, i
3. d	3. a, d, f
4. c	4. c, g

Essay Solutions

1. Modern psychoanalysis tends to be briefer (and therefore less expensive), less intense, and more flexible than classic techniques. For example, to accelerate the process, many analysts sit face-to-face with their clients and take a more active, engaging conversational role rather than relying on long-term free association. However, many aspects of Freud's original approach remain, including the emphasis on the importance of past experiences and unconscious processes, and the use of resistance and transference. (pp. 557-558)

2. Systematic desensitization is designed to condition people to respond to a feared stimulus, like a spider, with calmness rather than with anxiety. There are three basic procedures in systematic desensitization. The first step involves relaxation training. You will teach Toby how to relax the muscle groups throughout his body in response to a cue from you.

Next, you will help Toby to create an anxiety hierarchy; this is defined as a graduated sequence of fear-provoking situations that are rated on a 100-point scale from mild ("You see a photograph of a spider's web") to terrifying ("A large, hairy spider is crawling on your arm"). Finally, you will talk Toby into a state of relaxation and then guide him through a gradual series of exposures to these fear-provoking situations. As soon as he is able to remain relaxed while visualizing a particular situation, you will move him onto the next one. This routine will last for several sessions (probably). For long-term success, you will also want to use *in vivo exposure*, which involves having Toby actually confront the feared situations in real life. (pp. 559, 562-563)

3. A token economy is a large-scale reinforcement program in which individuals earn "tokens" for engaging in desired behaviors. For example, a developmentally disabled individual might receive a token every time he or she remembers to put away his or her clothing before bedtime, an anorexic client might receive a token for every ounce of weight he or she gains, and a hospitalized child might receive a token for participating in physical therapy sessions. These tokens then can be exchanged for various resources (e.g., candy, movie passes, play time). (p. 564)

Yes, punishment is sometimes necessary to eliminate dangerous or self-destructive behavior (p. 565). For example, a squirt of water from a spray bottle may be used to stop autistic children from injuring themselves by banging their heads against the wall.

4. The humanistic approach has four main features: (1) Trust is placed on the client's "growth" instincts; (2) the focus is upon feelings and not cognitions or behavior; (3) the orientation is toward the here-and-now rather than toward the past; and (4) the client is believed to be responsible for his or her own change (p. 571).

Person-centered therapy tends to be a "nicer" experience than Gestalt therapy. By this, I mean that the therapist's whole focus is upon creating a warm and caring relationship with the client that fosters self-exploration and discovery. To do this, the therapist offers unconditional positive regard, exhibits empathy, is genuine (honest and sincere), and uses nondirective reflection. Gestalt therapists also are interested in self-discovery, but they are more directive, less reflective, and brutally honest (the client is on the "hot seat"). (pp. 571-572)

5. Drug therapies definitely have positive effects. They have been used successfully to treat a variety of disorders, ranging from depression to bipolar disorder to some of the symptoms of schizophrenia. However, some drugs produce negative physical side effects (and even fatal illnesses) and some produce physical and psychological dependence. More worrisome is the fact that drugs do not deal with underlying problems – if someone's depression, for example, is due to an unresolved childhood conflict, then the depression is likely to return as soon as the client stops taking the drug. A more effective therapeutic strategy might be to use drugs in conjunction with psychotherapy. For example, antidepressants might increase a depressed person's level of functioning to the point where he or she is able to benefit from cognitive and behavioral therapies. (pp. 584-585)

CHAPTER 15

APPLYING PSYCHOLOGY

CHAPTER OVERVIEW

The final chapter in your text considers how psychologists apply what they learn in the laboratory to human problems. First the chapter considers the relationship between stress and health. The chapter considers the causes of stress, including catastrophes, major life events, and microstressors. The short-term and long-term physiological consequences of stress are examined (e.g., general adaptation syndrome, coronary heart disease, immune system malfunction), as are the various ways that people cope with stress (e.g., thought suppression, relaxation). The chapter then discusses personality factors (e.g., optimism) and social factors (social support) that appear to act as buffers against the harmful effects of stress. The next section of the chapter looks at how psychology can be applied to the legal system. Several sources of bias to jury decision-making are discussed including pretrial publicity and inadmissible evidence. Then the limitations of eyewitness testimony are considered, including the question of whether children make good eyewitnesses. The chapter next discusses confession evidence and the circumstances under which people may confess to crimes they did not commit. The next section of the chapter looks at the application of psychology to the workplace. The study of leadership is discussed as is motivation at work. The differences between intrinsic and extrinsic motivation are explained. The chapter ends with a discussion of equity theory.

CHAPTER OUTLINE

I. *What's Your Prediction* Does Stress Lower Resistance?

II. Stress and Health

    A. The Stress Response

    B. The Physiological Effects of Stress
        1. Effects of stress on the heart
        2. What stress does to the immune system
        3. The links between stress and illness

    C. *The Process of Discovery* Janice Kiecolt-Glaser

    D. Coping With Stress
        1. Thought suppression
        2. Relaxation
        3. Hope and optimism

        4. Optimism and hope
        5. Social support

   E. *Psychology and ?* Are Placebo Effects "All in the Mind"?

III. Psychology in the Law

   A. Jury Decision-Making
        1. Pretrial Publicity
        2. Inadmissible Evidence

   B. Eyewitness Testimony
        1. What influences lineup identifications?
        2. Are child witnesses competent to testify?

   C. Confession Evidence
        1. Police interrogations
        2. Lie-detector tests

IV. Psychology in the Workplace

   A. The Hawthorne Effect

   B. Leadership

   C. Motivation at Work
        a. Intrinsic and extrinsic motivation
        b. Equity motivation

V. Thinking Like a Psychologist About Applying Psychology

LEARNING OBJECTIVES

By the time you have read and reviewed this chapter, you should be able to:

1. Identify the basic focus of health psychology and explain why health has become a topic of interest for psychologists in recent years (p. 593).

2. Explain the main sources of stress, including catastrophes, major life events, and daily hassels or microstressors (pp. 594-595).

3. Describe the symptoms of posttraumatic stress disorder. Consider how common this problem is.

4. Describe the short-term and long-term effects of stress and define general adaptation syndrome (pp. 595-597).

5. Examine the relation between stress and coronary heart disease (pp. 597-598). Distinguish between a Type A and a Type B personality, and consider the relation between Type A behavior and coronary heart disease (pp. 597-598).

6. Explain the goals behind the field of psychoneuroimmunology (p. 599) and discuss the research evidence that shows that stress affects the immune system (pp. 599-600). Examine the relation between stress and physical illness (pp. 600-602).

7. Explain the difference between problem-focused, emotion-focused, and proactive coping (p. 603). Describe thought suppression and focused self-distraction as coping strategies (pp. 603-604).

8. Discuss the management of the physical symptoms of stress using relaxation (pp. 604-605).

9. Discuss the "self-healing personality" (p. 605). Consider optimism and its relation to coping with stress (pp. 605-606).

10. Discuss the placebo effect and explain how positive expectations may reduce anxiety and trigger physiological responses (p. 607).

11. Explain the relation between social support and psychological and physical health (pp. 608-609). Discuss why social support has beneficial consequences (pp. 608-609).

12. Discuss two sources of bias in the legal system (i.e., pretrial publicity, inadmissible evidence) (pp. 610-611).

13. Discuss the factors that may impair or influence eyewitness memory for events (e.g., emotional arousal, presence of a weapon) (p. 611). Explain how memories can be transformed by post-event information (pp. 611-612).

14. Consider the factors that influence lineup identifications (pp. 612-613). Discuss the impact of eyewitness confidence on juror judgments (p. 613).

15. Consider whether children are competent to provide eyewitness testimony (pp. 613-615). Explain the factors that can bias a child's memory report (p. 615).

16. Discuss the circumstances under which innocent suspects might give a false confession (pp. 615-616).

17. Explain what a polygraph is and how this instrument works (p. 617). Discuss whether the polygraph truly is a "lie detector" (pp. 617-618).

18. Describe the Hawthorne Effect (p. 618). Explain the importance of the discovery of this phenomena (p. 619).

19. Identify two approaches to studying leadership (p. 619). Describe the characteristics of a "natural born" leader (p. 619).

20. Discuss how external rewards may be used to motivate people at work. Specifically, consider expectancy theory and how it has been used to explain and predict worker attendance, productivity, and other job-related activities (p. 620).

21. Compare the concepts of intrinsic and extrinsic motivation (pp. 620-621). Explain how external rewards can reduce intrinsic motivation (p. 621). Discuss how the interpretation placed on an external reward (e.g., money), as well as the perceived fairness of that reward, may influence motivation (pp. 621-622).

22. Explain how equity theory accounts for work motivation and for behavior in the workplace (pp. 622-623).

KEY TERMS

The following key terms and concepts are featured in this chapter and are important for you to know. Write out definitions of each term and check your answers with the definitions in the text on the pages listed.

Psychoneuroimmunology (p. 592)
Health psychology (p. 593)
Stress (p. 594)
Posttraumatic stress disorder (PTSD) (p. 594)
General adaptation syndrome (p. 597)
Type A personality (p. 597)
Type B personality (p. 597)
Immune system (p. 598)
Lymphocytes (p. 598)
Social support (p. 608)
Polygraph (p. 616)
Hawthorne effect (p. 619)
Intrinsic motivation (p. 620)
Extrinsic motivation (p. 620)
Equity theory (p. 622)

TEST QUESTIONS

Multiple-Choice Questions

Circle the correct choice for each question and compare your answers with those at the end of the Study Guide chapter.

1. Psychoneuroimmunology is a new field that focuses on _____.
    a. the relation between personality factors and mental health
    b. the development of antipsychotic drug therapies
    c. the relation between the immune system and psychotic personality tendencies
    d. the association between physical and mental health

2. An unpleasant state of arousal that we experience in response to threatening events is defined as _____.
    a. anxiety
    b. stress
    c. reactance
    d. coping

3. Three months after Warren and Deb moved to California they lost their house in a major earthquake. Now, Warren is having problems sleeping at night and Deb frequently finds herself thinking about the original moments of the earthquake. What are Warren and Deb experiencing?
    a. posttraumatic stress disorder
    b. personal stressors
    c. psychosomatic disorder
    d. catastrophic flashbacks

4. Stressors may include
    a. catastrophes.
    b. major life events.
    c. daily hassles.
    d. All of the above

5. To assess a person's risk for developing coronary heart disease, you might ask him or her which of the following questions?
    a. "Do you smoke?"
    b. "Do you have high blood pressure and/or high cholesterol?"
    c. "Are you often under stress?"
    d. All of the above

6. Nan works hard at all that she does. She is impatient and competitive with her coworkers and friends, and often feels frustrated and hostile when she is unable to meet her goals. Nan's actions reflect _____.
   a. hardiness
   b. Type A personality
   c. Type B personality
   d. defense mechanisms

7. When Jim sees the work schedule for December, he realizes that he will be unable to go home and see his family during the holidays. "Oh well," he says, "There's a silver lining in every cloud. This will give me more time to work on the house." Jim is using _____ to deal with his stressful situation.
   a. emotion-focused coping
   b. social support
   c. problem-focused coping
   d. defense mechanisms

8. Julie also sees that she is scheduled to work over the holidays. However, she seeks out the boss and asks that her schedule be changed to accommodate her travel plans. Julie is using _____ to deal with her stressful situation.
   a. emotion-focused coping
   b. social support
   c. problem-focused coping
   d. defense mechanisms

9. What are the physiological effects of meditation
   a. slower breathing
   b. drop in the amount of lactate in the blood
   c. slower brain wave patterns
   d. all of the above

10. Francis did not get the lead in the school play, even though he practiced his lines every day for a month before auditions. "Oh well," he says, "the director must have thought that the other guy would be better for this particular part. I'll get the next one." Francis is a(n)
    a. pessimist.
    b. optimist.
    c. Type A personality.
    d. Type B personality.

11. Optimists tend to attribute their successes to _____ factors and their failures to
    _____ factors.
    a. external; internal
    b. temporary; stable
    c. internal; external
    d. specific; global

12. A placebo is able to improve someone's condition by
    a. altering the physical structure of the brain.
    b. increasing the rate of neurotransmitter activity.
    c. providing the suggestion that he or she will improve.
    d. decreasing physiological arousal.

13. Placebos have been used successfully to treat
    a. allergies.
    b. headaches.
    c. chronic pain.
    d. All of the above

14. Positive expectations about a particular treatment may trigger the release of _____.
    a. anxiety
    b. endorphins
    c. dopamine
    d. glucose

15. Carmen also did not get the lead in the school play, and he practiced even harder than did
    Francis. His friends tell him that he did not succeed because the director was new and
    didn't know what he was doing. Carmen listens to his friends and now feels better about
    himself. His friends provided _____.
    a. social support
    b. optimistic support
    c. emotion-focused coping
    d. hardiness

16. Which of the following individuals can provide social support?
    a. a relative
    b. a friend
    c. a family member
    d. All of the above

17. Possible sources of bias in the court system include
    a. jurors' exposure to pretrial publicity.
    b. jurors' exposure to admissible evidence.
    c. the physical attractiveness of the jurors.
    d. All of the above

18. Research shows that people who know a lot about a case from TV and newspaper coverage are
    a. more likely to presume the defendant guilty
    b. less likely to presume the defendant guilty
    c. more likely to believe they can be impartial
    d. none of the above

19. Schara was a witness to a minor car accident. When the police officer arrived at the scene he interviewed her and asked questions such as, "How fast were the cars going when they smashed each other?" How might the wording of this question affect Schara's memory of the event?
    a. It could cause her to believe the cars were going slower than they actually were.
    b. It could cause her to believe the cars were going faster than they actually were.
    c. It could cause her to believe that there was no broken glass present when there actually was broken glass.
    d. All of the above

20. The polygraph enables psychologists to _____.
    a. detect deception
    b. measure the expressive component of emotions
    c. assess brain activity
    d. record physiological arousal

21. The use of the polygraph is based on the assumption that people who are being deceptive experience _____.
    a. pupil dilation
    b. increased brain activity
    c. increased autonomic arousal
    d. decreased activity in the left hemisphere and increased activity in the right hemisphere

22. In the studies at the Hawthorne plant, which of the following changes increased productivity?
    a. changing the illumination
    b. adding an additional rest period
    c. providing a free midmorning lunch
    d. all of the above

23. In the Hawthorne studies why did being asked to work in the test room affect workers productivity?
    a. They were motivated by extra money.
    b. They enjoyed the attention of being studied.
    c. They were worried they would lose their jobs.
    d. They were embarrassed by the extra attention.

24. Good leadership is all about _____.
    a. controlling resources
    b. cooperation
    c. social influence
    d. problem solving

25. Situationally oriented theories are based on the notion that the emergence of a given leader depends on
    a. the time
    b. the place
    c. the circumstances
    d. all of the above

26. According to expectancy theory, people are _____ decision makers who work hard when they expect that their efforts will improve their own performance and increase their rewards.
    a. selfish
    b. rational
    c. competitive
    d. irrational

27. William teaches high school because he enjoys working with young adults and he believes in the value of education. He finds the job challenging and always stimulating. Buddy teaches high school because he enjoys the summer vacation schedule and he wants to attain tenure and job security. William is _____ motivated; Buddy is _____ motivated.
    a. intrinsically; extrinsically
    b. extrinsically; intrinsically
    c. internally; expectantly
    d. extrinsically; extrinsically

28. Sheila wants to increase her workers' productivity by giving them bonuses (monetary incentives). These rewards are likely to have a positive effect if they
    a. are perceived as a means of controlling worker productivity.
    b. enhance extrinsic but not intrinsic motivation.
    c. are perceived as a source of information about performance quality.
    d. All of the above.

29. According to equity theory, people who feel that they are being underpaid for their work will experience _____ distress compared to those who feel that they are being overpaid for their work.
    a. slightly more
    b. less
    c. significantly more
    d. equal

30. Gerald feels that he is being underpaid for all the work he does. How can he relieve his distress at this situation and restore equity?
    a. He can work fewer hours and/or be less productive.
    b. He can seek to obtain a raise.
    c. He can convince himself that equity already exists.
    d. All of the above

True-False Questions

Indicate which of the following statements are true or false, and compare your answers with those at the end of the chapter.

T   F   1. Once we are infected, stress appears to lower our resistance to illness.

T   F   2. Small daily hassles may contribute more to stress and illness than major life events.

T   F   3. People who are hostile exhibit more intense cardiovascular reactions only during the event that makes them angry.

T   F   4. Relaxation can fortify the immune system.

T   F   5. The placebo effect is not a purely mental phenomenon.

T   F   6. Any supportive relationship may contribute to our mental and physical health.

T   F   7. Eyewitnesses's confidence can be raised and lowered by external factors.

T   F   8. Innocent people cannot be induced to confess.

T   F   9. Transformational leaders motivate followers to transcend their personal needs in the interest of a common cause.

T   F   10. To be maximally productive, people should feel externally driven.

Key Concepts Matching Exercises

Exercise #1: Applied Psychology

Match the phenomena listed on the left with the examples listed on the right.

_____ 1. Intrinsic motivation

_____ 2. Extrinsic motivation

_____ 3. Equity

_____ 4. Pessimism

_____ 5. Optimism

_____ 6. Posttraumatic stress disorder

_____ 7. General adaptation syndrome

_____ 8. Type A personality

_____ 9. Type B personality

a. "Why are people so slow? I can't wait any longer. I have things to do, places to go, people to see. Let's move it, folks!"

b. "I try to look at the bright side of life. When things go well, I know that it's because I made them happen. When things don't go well, it's probably just a fluke and won't happen again."

c. "At first, I was really energized. My body and mind were so aroused and alert. But after a few weeks, I got really worn out. Now, I can't seem to shake this cold I picked up."

d. "It makes sense that Shawna earns more than I do; after all, she puts in more hours. We both get out what we put in."

e. "Oh, I don't mind waiting. It'll give me a chance to relax. After all, we all need to stop and smell the flowers once in a while."

f. "I'll work the overtime because I love the job so much. I don't care if I get paid extra."

g. "Face it, the glass is always half empty. I didn't get the raise because I'm doomed to failure. They only hired me in the first place because they were desperate; it certainly wasn't because of my qualifications."

h. "I'll work the overtime, but only if I get a bonus."

i. "Ever since the flood, I've been unable to sleep, I feel anxious all the time, and I keep having these horrible flashbacks."

Essay Questions

Write out answers to the following brief essay questions. Compare your responses with the sample answers at the end of the Study Guide chapter.

1. Diana just moved to a new town and started an extremely challenging job. On the first day of her new job, what immediate reactions might she experience? What long-term reactions might she experience? Discuss the circumstances under which her reactions may be beneficial or harmful (include Selye's general adaptation syndrome in your discussion).

2. Explain the difference between problem-focused coping and emotion-focused coping.

3. Charles is experiencing a great deal of stress in his daily life. He knows you are taking a psychology course and asks for your advice on ways that he might more effectively reduce or manage his level of stress. What will you tell him?

4. A prominent attorney calls you to ask for advice. It seems that her client has been accused of selling his company's computer software ideas to a rival development corporation. Her client wants to take a polygraph test to prove his innocence. What will you tell the attorney?

5. Alex needs to increase worker productivity. She has decided to implement a "pay-for-performance" program in which workers will receive a monetary reward for every extra client they bring in to the company. These rewards will be tracked, and a plaque will be awarded to the most productive employee at the end of each month. Knowing that you are a brilliant psychologist, Alex turns to you for some last minute advice about how to implement her program. What will you tell her?

TEST SOLUTIONS

Multiple-Choice Solutions

1.	d (p. 592)	11.	c (p. 605)	21.	c (p. 617)
2.	b (p. 594)	12.	c (p. 607)	22.	d (p. 618)
3.	a (p. 594)	13.	d (p. 607)	23.	b (p. 619)
4.	d (p. 595)	14.	b (p. 607)	24.	c (p. 619)
5.	d (p. 597)	15.	a (p. 608)	25.	d (p. 619)
6.	b (p. 597)	16.	d (p. 608)	26.	b (p. 620)
7.	a (p. 603)	17.	a (p. 610)	27.	a (pp. 620-621)
8.	c (p. 603)	18.	a (p. 610)	28.	c (p. 622)
9.	d (p. 604)	19.	b (p. 611)	29.	d (p. 622)
10.	b (p. 605)	20.	d (p. 617)	30.	d (p. 622)

True-False Solutions

1.	T (p. 592)	6.	T (p. 608)
2.	T (p. 595)	7.	T (p. 613)
3.	F (p. 598)	8.	F (p. 616)
4.	T (p. 604)	9.	T (p. 620)
5.	T (p. 607)	10.	F (p. 621)

Key Concepts Matching Solutions

Exercise #1

1. f
2. h
3. d
4. g
5. b
6. i
7. c
8. a
9. e

Essay Solutions

1. According to Selye, Diana will first experience an "alarm" reaction to any stressor. This reaction includes a rise in heart rate, blood pressure, and breathing rate, and the secretion of certain adrenal gland hormones. In the short term, these physiological reactions may be beneficial or adaptive. For example, Diana may experience a burst of energy that helps her to cope with her job's challenges. If the stress continues over time, however, she may experience deterioration of body tissues due to the ongoing secretion of stress-related hormones (this occurs during the "resistance" stage, when the body remains aroused and alert). Over time, Diana may become more susceptible to disease and illness, either because her antistress resources are limited or because the overuse of these resources has caused other systems in her body to break down (this is referred to as the "exhaustion" phase, according to Selye's model). In general, then, reactions to long-term, sustained stress are harmful. (p. 596)

2. Problem-focused coping is designed to reduce stress by overcoming the source of the problem. For example, if you were having difficulty with a class, you might seek out a school counselor, your academic adviser, your course professor, and people you knew had successfully passed that particular class. In other words, you go to the root of the problem itself. Emotion-focused coping does not focus on the source of the problem, but rather on the emotional aftermath of the problem. For example, if your class was causing you to feel anxious and depressed, you might decide to simply tough it out and make the best of the situation, hoping that you would feel better at the end of the term. Problem-focused coping is more likely to occur when we feel that we can actually control the situation; emotion-focused coping is more likely in situations that we feel cannot be controlled. (p. 603)

3. Charles has several options available to him. As noted in the answer to the previous question, he can employ problem-focused coping and reduce his stress level by removing the source of stress, and he can also employ emotion-focused coping strategies (including thought suppression and focused self-distraction) to manage his emotional response to a stressor (pp. 603-604). He can also manage the physical symptoms of stress by taking a class in relaxation training (pp. 604-605). Charles might also use or learn to use an "optimistic" explanatory style. For example, he could learn to blame failures on external, temporary, and specific factors, and to credit successes to internal, permanent, and global factors (p. 605). Finally, he could seek out social support and ask for assistance from caring others (pp. 608-609).

4. Well, the first thing you will tell her is to make sure that she, her client, and the company realize that the polygraph is not a "lie-detector" in and of itself. All that the instrument does is to record physiological arousal. When combined with an oral examination, a naive subject, and a well-trained examiner, the test may in fact do a decent job of revealing deception or truth. However, there are some important considerations that the attorney (and her client) should keep in mind. First, it is possible for a truthful person to actually "fail" the test; that is, her client may be telling the truth, but his level of arousal

may indicate that he is "lying." Second, the test can be "faked." People can inflate their arousal level (by tensing their muscles, biting their tongues, etc.) during the control question portion of the exam; this will give them a higher baseline of arousal, so that any arousal that they experience during the crime-relevant question portion will not appear unduly high. Therefore, perhaps her client should reconsider whether he wants to base his entire defense on a polygraph test! (pp. 617-618)

5. First, you need to make sure that she is aware of the possible negative consequences of using monetary (and other) rewards as incentives for production. If her employees already enjoy bringing clients into the firm and find their jobs to be satisfying (in other words, they have high intrinsic motivation), then providing an external reward may actually inhibit productivity. The reward may alter their perceptions of the task of soliciting clients; it may come to be seen as "work" and not "fun" (pp. 620-621).

However, there are ways to present a monetary reward that increase the likelihood that it will be successful. Specifically, if Alex offers the payment in a way that her employees feel is manipulative and designed to control and bribe them (e.g., "I'll be watching you," "You'd better produce or else"), her efforts are probably doomed to fail. She should take great care to frame the reward as a source of information; for example, she might inform her employees that "these rewards are a way for you all to monitor your own progress and the quality of your performance." Also, the reward should be presented in a positive manner, as a tangible form of praise for a job well done (pp. 621-622).